THE
BOOK
OF
CALM

250 WAYS TO
A CALMER YOU

Adams Media

New York   London   Toronto   Sydney   New Delhi

Aadamsmedia

Adams Media
An Imprint of Simon & Schuster, Inc.
57 Littlefield Street
Avon, Massachusetts 02322

First Adams Media trade paperback edition December 2018

ADAMS MEDIA and colophon are trademarks of Simon & Schuster.

For information about special discounts for bulk purchases, please contact Simon & Schuster Special Sales at 1-866-506-1949 or business@simonandschuster.com.

The Simon & Schuster Speakers Bureau can bring authors to your live event. For more information or to book an event contact the Simon & Schuster Speakers Bureau at 1-866-248-3049 or visit our website at www.simonspeakers.com.

Interior design by Erin Alexander

Manufactured in the United States of America

10 9 8 7 6 5 4 3 2

Library of Congress Cataloging-in-Publication Data has been applied for.

ISBN 978-1-5072-1005-5
ISBN 978-1-5072-1006-2 (ebook)

Contains material adapted from the following titles published by Adams Media, an Imprint of Simon & Schuster, Inc.: *My Pocket Meditations* by Meera Lester, copyright © 2017, ISBN 978-1-5072-0341-5; *My Pocket Guru* by Adams Media, copyright © 2016, ISBN 978-1-4405-9246-1; *Meditation Made Easy* by Preston Bentley, copyright © 2015, ISBN 978-1-4405-8432-9; *Mantras Made Easy* by Sherianna Boyle, MEd, CAGS, copyright © 2017, ISBN 978-1-4405-9997-2; *5-Minute Mindfulness* by David Dillard-Wright, PhD, Heidi E. Spear, and Paula Munier, copyright © 2012, ISBN 978-1-4405-2979-5; *Stress Less* by Kate Hanley, copyright © 2017, ISBN 978-1-5072-0193-0; *Meditation for Moms* by Kim Dwyer and Susan Reynolds, copyright © 2012, ISBN 978-1-4405-3027-2; *An Indulgence a Day* by Andrea Norville and Patrick Menton, copyright © 2009, ISBN 978-1-60550-152-9.

Introduction

Being calm is about finding a moment of quiet in the chaos of everyday life. Slowing down, taking a breath, and embracing peace can all help give you a new perspective on your day, and help you be ready for the challenges that may come your way. And while finding tranquility in today's hectic world can be a struggle, *The Book of Calm* gives you what you need to find peace, no matter the situation.

Throughout the book you'll find 250 ways to fill yourself with a feeling of peace, calm, and well-being, including:

- Inspirational quotes
- Breathing exercises
- Yoga poses
- Meditations
- Mantras
- And more...

From taking a mindful shower to doing some deep breathing, the ideas in this book will give you the tools to invite calm right now, whether you're preparing to do something that scares you, trying to keep your cool in the middle of a tough conversation, or just looking for a breather after a hard day.

If you struggle to find serenity in the midst of a busy, stressful life, don't worry. *The Book of Calm* has just what you need to stop, breathe, and calm yourself down—any time you need it.

Say *Ahhhhh*

Open your mouth wide, take a deep breath, and breathe out a calming *ahhhhh*. This simple sound is far more powerful than you may think. You're giving yourself permission to release tension in your neck, your shoulders, or anywhere else. Muscle tension is often a reflection of energy that is being held hostage in the body, and can keep you sore and on edge. Circulating fresh oxygen deep into your body helps you release this pent-up energy. Go ahead, fill up your belly with breath. Inflate it now, fully (like a balloon). Allow your mouth to open slightly and release a nice *ahhhhh* sound.

Practice Walking

Walking is something most of us learn to do when we're very little, and then we don't think much about it. Taking a moment to slow down and just focus on walking can be a soothing, meditative activity if you're feeling overwhelmed.

1. When you begin a walking meditation, pretend that you have never walked before. It helps to practice in your home with bare feet before trying this outdoors.
2. Create a clear path, maybe a hallway, or any place in your home where you can walk back and forth.
3. Focus on your posture, straightening your spine from your tailbone to the crown of your head, and standing squarely over your feet and hips.
4. Feel your feet on the floor. Imagine that your feet have never touched or felt the floor, like you're on another planet and have no idea how this "new ground" will feel. Notice every inch of your feet touching the floor or the ground. Be curious about how everything feels under your feet.
5. Lengthen your body up through your spine to the crown of your head. Bring your shoulders down and back to open your heart center. Make sure your chin is slightly tucked.
6. Take small steps, and step lightly and slowly. Smile while you are walking. Realize how different it is to walk without having a place to go and how refreshing it feels to be focused solely on walking, surrendering all thought about anything other than walking.

Get In Touch with Yourself

Whenever you need to calm down, rest your hand on your stomach or your heart to draw your focus down, away from your head and its litany of thoughts, and into your body, where you are always in the present moment and where your inner peace resides. It's a small movement—so small, you can do it even in a meeting or while riding a crowded train—with big results because it helps you use your whole being to handle whatever stressor is at your door.

✦

If you want to conquer the anxiety of life, live in the moment, live in the breath.

—AMIT RAY
Indian spiritual teacher and author

Try the Sippy Straw Exercise

Here's a quickie breathing exercise that will revive you and help you feel calm. Many of us are not breathing fully; we have old breath swirling in our lungs. Most of us only use about a quarter of our lung capacity. When you fully exhale, you create space to bring new and fresh breath to your lungs. This full breath will release serotonin, a hormone associated with happiness, and create a feeling of peace.

1. Pretend you are breathing through a straw. Inhale little sips of breath without exhaling. Sip in as much breath as you can. Fill all five lobes of your lungs with breath, until you cannot sip anymore, and then exhale out of your mouth.
2. When you exhale and think you are done exhaling, exhale some more. This is energizing, as well as soothing, so it should not be done in the early evening, as it will keep you awake.

Draw Peace from the Earth

Many Eastern philosophies, including nature-based spiritual paths, embrace the idea of showing kindness to all living beings, nature, and planet earth. You can draw peace and calm from the earth with this simple meditation. Try it while lying on your back on a yoga mat or on a folded blanket on the ground.

1. Lie on your back with a long spine and with your legs straight out and your arms resting at your sides (in yoga, this is called Corpse Pose).
2. Release your worries, stress, and tension and give them over to the power of the earth and the energy that created the earth and the life that lives on it.
3. Breathe in and visualize waves of peaceful energy flowing into your spine and radiating out to all parts of your body, spreading peace and healing energies through your head, torso, arms, and legs, and through every cell in your body.
4. Breathe out, feeling gratitude while visualizing all of that energy soaking back into the earth.

◆

Look at a tree,
a flower, a plant.
Let your awareness
rest upon it.
How still they are,
how deeply rooted in
Being. Allow nature
to teach you stillness.

—ECKHART TOLLE
German-born spiritual teacher and author

Sculpt with Play-Doh

You probably spent more time squeezing and squashing Play-Doh than making sculptures when you were a kid. It smelled funny, but it was magical in its own way. Now that you're a bit older, you can still have fun molding Play-Doh into jungle animals or flowers, and knead your stress away as you work with the dough. Buy a few jars and create a wonderful sculpture. Or you can make your own dough by combining flour, water, salt, vegetable oil, and a little food dye.

Take an Energy Shower

If you've been around people whose negative energy has rubbed off on you, or you're sending out some stressful, negative energy yourself, take an energy-cleansing "shower" to banish the bad energy and invite in some calm.

1. Stand and imagine you have removed your clothing. Brush your arms briskly (but gently!) and picture the dust of stress flying off you and away. Inhale and reach your arms up above your head.
2. Exhale and lower your arms to your sides, imagining a shower of sparkling gold light trickling over your body, spreading from your head to your toes.
3. Repeat the motion several times, allowing this gold light to cascade over your body and clean all of the stress and negative energy you may be feeling or may have picked up during the day. Visualize the negative energy flowing away from you and being absorbed by the earth. As the negative energy drips away, feel peace flow in to take its place.

Call a Friend

Daily life can be hectic, filled with a million little stressors, and we all need the support of a cherished relationship from time to time. A great way to find some perspective and a feeling of peace is to call up a trusted friend, with whom you can speak candidly and truthfully, someone who is caring and has a genuine concern for your needs and feelings and has a sense of humor. It feels so great to be able to laugh at yourself and not take yourself too seriously! A true friend will encourage, accept, and support you, no matter what is happening in your life. We all have a need for authentic friendship, to receive it and to give it as well. Keep these tips in mind when you place your call:

- Make sure you are comfortable, maybe with your feet elevated and a cup of tea within reach.
- Don't use the phone call as an opportunity to vent; think of it as a meditation, a talking meditation that helps you relieve stress and feel grounded.
- Choose to mindfully talk with your friend, asking for her support during a stressful time, mindfully connecting with someone who understands and cares about you.

✦

People become attached to their burdens sometimes more than the burdens are attached to them.

—GEORGE BERNARD SHAW
Irish playwright

Take a Breather

The life force or living energy that connects to all that there is and sustains our life breath is called *ki* in Japanese; the Chinese refer to it as *chi*, while the Hindus call it *prana*. The following exercise helps to open up your ki passages. Focusing on your breath can allow you to let go of anxieties and fears that are keeping your breath shallow. It helps you to physically release tension, and gives you a mental focal point for keeping yourself calm.

1. Sit upright with your spine straight.
2. Open your mouth, relax your jaw, stick out your tongue, and pant like a dog.
3. Continue for several minutes. These in-and-out breaths will open up your belly and clear the energy passageways from the base of your spine to your throat's vocal cords.

Use a Mudra

You may have seen pictures of people meditating with their legs crossed and their hands in a certain position. That's what doing a *mudra* looks like. Mudras are hand gestures often used to complement a mantra or meditation practice, and they are powerful means for connecting to a higher consciousness. You can use a mudra to add some extra oomph to your own meditation practice, or use the hand gesture to create a moment of peace during your day. One simple mudra you can try is similar to the "okay" sign: take your pointer finger and press it against your thumb. This is a universal mudra that represents the universal soul connecting with the individual soul.

Write a Haiku

A haiku is a three-line poem that many people use as a meditation aid. They can also just be a lot of fun to compose. Creating art is a great way to slow down and get in touch with your inner self. The specific structure (based on syllable count) and brevity of the haiku poem also helps to keep you even more focused and mindful as you write.

1. To write a haiku in English, concentrate on simply capturing a fleeting moment, evoking a beautiful image of the ephemeral quality of life.
2. A haiku often focuses on a moment in nature, and typically includes a word that lets the reader know what season it is. For example, the word *daffodils* would indicate spring.
3. Here's a good structure to use when you first start writing haiku: five syllables in the first line, seven in the second line, and five in the last line. Read several haiku first, so you can get a sense of their rhythm and tone.
4. It's traditional in Japanese haiku to use a *kireji*, or a cutting word. This word is used to show juxtaposition between two ideas in the haiku, or to signal the end of one of the images. In English, it's typically done with a punctuation mark, like a dash or period, since our language works differently.
5. Share your haiku with family and friends. Post them in your cubicle at work or on your fridge at home. Use them as a focus during your meditation exercises.

Use Your Breath to Take a Break

Try this breathing pattern for ten breaths:

1. Inhale normally. Exhale normally.
2. Pause. Begin the next breath before you feel desperate for air (meaning, a bigger pause isn't necessarily better).

The beauty of this technique is that it elbows out room for you to rest—to reflect before you make your next move. And that's when you start making decisions that reduce your stress instead of adding to it. Also, no one will notice you're doing it, which means you can practice this breathing anywhere—your desk, the dentist's chair, or even in the midst of a difficult conversation.

Shake It Off

Sometimes when stress or negativity just won't go away, you can get rid of it by literally shaking (or flinging or flailing) it off your body. Physical actions can be a very present and effective way to act out changes you want to make. This is a great, short exercise for shaking off your negativity so you have room to embrace calm.

1. Stand up where you are and feel your feet firmly on the ground.
2. Lift one foot at a time and shake your leg while you inhale and exhale three times for each leg. If balancing is hard for you, hold on to the back of a chair so you don't fall.
3. After you shake out both legs, shake out your arms for three long breaths.

✦

Stop a minute,
right where you are.
Relax your shoulders,
shake your head and
spine like a dog
shaking off cold
water. Tell that
imperious voice in
your head to be still.

—BARBARA KINGSOLVER
American author

Banish Negative Thoughts

Sometimes you find yourself inundated by negative thoughts that crowd out your calm and leave you stressed. When that happens, try this calming meditation. You can even do this exercise at work on days your stress leaves you feeling overwhelmed. It allows you to acknowledge your thoughts and then dismiss them, freeing up space for peaceful and positive thoughts to enter your mind.

1. Sit in a straight-backed chair or cross-legged on the floor. Close your eyes and begin breathing deeply: eight counts in, hold four counts, eight counts out, hold four counts. Keep counting your breaths for four to six cycles. When you can maintain the same rhythm, let go of the counting.

2. Watch your thoughts. As they arise, dismiss them, silently saying *Not this* or *Not that*. Keep your negation simple without attaching any emotion or judgment to it. At the same time, keep your attitude expectant, as though you were waiting for something better than the thoughts your mind normally presents to you.

3. Continue dismissing your thoughts, one by one, for the rest of the session. Don't worry if you have trouble doing this; just keep trying. When you open your eyes, note any shifts in your perceptions.

Let Someone Brush Your Hair

You brush your hair every day, but it's a completely different experience when someone else does it for you. Ask a friend or partner to brush your hair. Have them use a large paddle brush so it makes your hair very soft. If they do it slowly and softly, it's sometimes enough to lull you to sleep. Offer to return the favor; even if they have short hair, they are sure to enjoy this wonderful sensation.

◆

Love is what we are born with. Fear is what we learn.

—MARIANNE WILLIAMSON
Spiritual teacher, author, and lecturer

Meditate On Your Root Chakra

If you are afraid or worried about something, you can get help from your root chakra. Chakras are areas of energy in your body, and the first chakra, the root chakra (located in the base of the spine), is the one related to stability and grounding. When you are anxious, your energy is predominantly up in your mind. Doing something physical, energizing the body, will bring energy down from the mind into the body.

1. If the weather permits, get outside to allow the earth's force to help ground you.
2. Whether or not you can get outside, breathe in and out slowly, gently, and deeply, feeling your body expand to allow the air to rush inward on the inhale.
3. Envision your connection to the earth; imagine your inhale going through your body into the ground. Create longer exhalation than inhalation to induce relaxation.
4. If you are standing up, imagine your legs as though they have roots growing deeply into the earth. Know you are rooted and connected. If you want to sit down on the ground or floor, then you can imagine the energy coming down from your head out through the root chakra into the earth.
5. For several minutes, breathe and envision energy coming down into the body and flowing into the earth.

Give Yourself a Pep Talk

Positive self-talk can go a long way in calming you down and helping you find peace in stressful situations, like when you have to give a presentation or speak in public. If you are nervous about speaking in front of a group of people, try repeating a positive phrase like "I am calm. I can do this." The words "I am" are some of the most powerful words you can use. Think of these words as putting into motion what it is you choose to create. In this case, you are activating calm by embracing nervousness. See yourself as improving and know, with practice, this fear can and will dissipate. Practice this phrase in front of a mirror and see how this strengthens you. Don't forget to breathe!

Create Something

Creating something new can be very soothing and fulfilling, no matter what it is you create. If you're feeling stressed, being creative can help you feel productive as you take a break from your to-do list. You can choose any creative project that speaks to you and that you enjoy: color in a coloring book, write in your journal, practice an instrument, paint with watercolors, sculpt with clay, or sing or dance to music. Go to a quiet place where you are unlikely to be disturbed, and start creating.

Try not to look at your creations or analyze your own performance right away. Once you've done this a few times, you can look back at your creations or activities and see if you spot any patterns. Words and images that recur in writing or painting or drawing are your personal themes. Movements or sounds can also have meaning for you, personally, if you are dancing or playing music. Spend some time meditating on what they could mean for you.

Peace is always beautiful.

—WALT WHITMAN
American poet

Light Some Incense

Incense imparts a feeling of the sacred and can support the atmosphere of meditation. Here are some suggestions for incense selections:

- For facilitating breath work: eucalyptus, pine, and lavender are clean and penetrating scents.
- For mental focus: basil, geranium, and frankincense penetrate deeply through the emotional sphere and have lasting power.
- For purifying emotions: jasmine, vetiver, sage, and cypress have a calming effect on mood.
- For neutralizing stress: rosemary reduces melancholy, and scents of the mint family (peppermint, spearmint) are mentally uplifting.
- For an inspirational atmosphere: patchouli, sandalwood, and myrrh are the traditional ingredients for liturgical incense.

Tree Bathe

The Japanese have a name for spending time among trees: *shinrin-yoku*, or "forest bathing," which has been shown to reduce stress and improve immunity. You can draw peace and comfort from the company of trees, whether they're in your yard, at your local park, or along a walking trail. The sound of rustling leaves, the woodsy scents, and the dappled light all soothe the soul in a major way—particularly when you use your powers of attention to really appreciate them. Hugging and climbing the trees are optional (but encouraged!).

◆

Step outside
for a while—calm
your mind. It is
better to hug a
tree than to bang
your head against
a wall continually.

—RASHEED OGUNLARU
English author and life coach

Say a Chant for Compassion

Pronounced as it is spelled, *Om Mani Padme Hum*, one of the most popular mantras in the world, is intended to create compassion. Many people will begin saying it and transition into singing it, formulating their own tune. Roughly translated, it means "When the heart and the mind get together and combine efforts, then anything is possible." So whenever you need some mantra mojo, try saying, then chanting (or singing) "Om Mani Padme Hum...Om Mani Padme Hum."

A yoga concept called *Naad* holds that the roof of your mouth has eighty-four meridian points (located along energy channels) that can be stimulated when your tongue strikes them, such as when speaking. According to Naad, the meridian points stimulate the hypothalamus gland, which stimulates the pineal gland, which stimulates the pituitary gland. The pituitary gland and the entire glandular system play a role in experiencing emotions and achieving bliss; this connection means that the sound of a word (and the meridian the tongue strikes while saying the word) is just as important as what the word means. Over thousands of years, yogis have created mantras designed to strike meridians that will facilitate a meditative state. *Om Mani Padme Hum!*

✦

A mantra truly is a vehicle that takes you into quieter, more peaceful levels of the mind.

—DEEPAK CHOPRA
Indian-American author and public speaker

Get a Massage

Getting a professional massage can be a great way to clear up negative energy that's been stressing you out, and give yourself a relaxing, pampered break. We hold a great deal of our tension in our bodies; a professional masseuse can soothe that tension and loosen up some of the fascia that's keeping you tied up tight. Getting a massage can soothe physical pain, and it can help you get into the mind-set of self-care: it feels good to take care of yourself and make your comfort a priority. Treating yourself to some hands-on care often serves as a reminder of the importance of taking a break once in a while, and it can help strengthen your resilience as you face down your daily challenges.

Have Your House Blessed

Before moving into a new place is the best time for a house blessing, but it will still work if you've lived there a while. If you're feeling stuck or stressed in your home, having it blessed can clear out that old, stale energy and open it up to more peaceful energies. Depending on what religion you subscribe to, you can have a priest or member of the clergy come to your home—or you can even try it yourself. Get some sage to burn as you walk around the house and through every room. Burning sage cleanses the room of any negative energy. You can then go room to room and say a prayer or just wish for happiness and peace while you live in the house.

Balance in Tree Pose

The Tree Pose yoga position is perfect physically and psychologically for dealing with daily stresses. It helps develop balance, steadiness, and poise, and helps you to feel grounded.

1. Stand with your feet hip-width apart. Feel the four corners of each foot pressing evenly into the floor. (It's great to do this pose outside with bare feet, weather permitting.)
2. Lengthen your spine, lift the crown of your head toward the ceiling (or sky if practicing outside), gently engage your leg muscles, and engage your abdomen by pulling the stomach muscles inward.
3. Bring the sole of your right foot against your supporting leg and open your knee out to the side. (Feel free to touch a chair or counter to help with balance.) Bring your hands together in a prayer position. Look at something that is not moving to help with balance, and focus on your breath until you feel steady.
4. Bring your hands up as though you were extending your branches. While in Tree Pose, think about what tree you resonate with today. Are you a willow tree, swaying back and forth, or are you an oak tree, standing firm and strong? How about a cherry or apple tree?

✦

Even the tallest trees are able to grow from tiny seeds like these. Remember this, and try not to rush time.

—PAULO COELHO
Brazilian lyricist and author

Face Unpleasant Chores
with Mindfulness

Approaching a task with mindfulness can help to make it less of a hassle, and gives you an opportunity to seek out a moment of Zen in your busy day. You can do anything mindfully; you can even clean a bathroom mindfully! Go slowly and let the way you approach this task set the tone for the rest of the day. Choose a nicely scented and organic product to clean the different surfaces. Pay attention to what you're doing, instead of trying to rush through it. Notice the judgments you make about the different areas of the bathroom, and about cleaning it. Recognize how much time you waste thinking about what you have to do, instead of simply accepting that it must be done and attending to it. Part of a meditation practice is acceptance. As you clean, focus on making the space clean, and think of it as a gift to yourself and your housemates. Imagine them noticing how delightful it feels to have a nicely scented and fresh bathroom to use.

Fight Fear with Breath

Here's the thing: fear is not real. When you are experiencing symptoms of fear it sure feels real, though, doesn't it? The way you see the world is affected when you are in fear and your energy is not circulating properly. Rather than seeing choices, you see limitations; rather than seeing love, you see hurt and resentment. If you are feeling fearful, take a few moments to connect with your breath. On the inhale, inflate your lower abdomen and take in one slow, rhythmic breath. Allow the energy of fear to transform into peace, courage, strength, and (with practice) love. As you are breathing, use this mantra: *Fear is an illusion. Love is the only thing that's real.* State this mantra three to five times and then take one full complete breath (inhale to the count of three and exhale to the count of three). Imagine these words as energy moving freely through your body.

Do Some Cooking Therapy

Preparing food can be very relaxing and can itself be a mindful meditation. Food is necessary to survive, and it can be powerful to take time to be mindful of that fact and grateful for our ability to provide for and support ourselves. This mindfulness meditation works best with recipes with lots of ingredients, like stir-fry, but you can use the same instructions for pausing, observing, and appreciating the different elements of whatever food you decide to make.

As you prepare vegetables, for example, stand with all of the vegetables laid out on the counter in front of you. Line up everything to chop. Make sure that you do this slowly and use all of your senses:

- Look at the colors of the vegetables: the bright orange of the carrots, the green of broccoli, or the white onion.
- Feel the vegetables: the texture, the softness of the silky threads of corn on the cob, the rough skin of carrots, or the bumpy eyes of a potato. When was the last time you really appreciated a vegetable?
- Taste a raw vegetable now and then as you are chopping, and really notice the texture and taste.
- Listen to the sound of the chopping and how it sounds different with each vegetable.

Take a moment to really appreciate and give gratitude to everyone who worked so that the food is available to you: the farmers and workers who harvest the food, the store clerk who sells the food, and to yourself, for making the effort to prepare yourself a meal that will nourish and sustain you.

Take a Nap

If your last nap was twenty to thirty years ago, take some time today for a quick nap. A quick thirty-minute midday nap has been proven to lessen stress, increase learning, and improve health. This may be hard if you are at work, but even closing your eyes for five minutes in your office is proven to relieve stress and give you a boost of energy. Those few moments will help you decompress and give your body the needed break it deserves. Be careful of napping for more than an hour, as you may have a hard time falling asleep that evening.

✦

Naps are nature's
way of reminding
you that life is nice—
like a beautiful,
softly swinging
hammock strung
between birth
and infinity.

—PEGGY NOONAN
American author

Count to 10

If you're stressing out and need a quick and easy meditation to calm yourself down, you can always count to 10. Many people feel they're "bad" at meditating, but if you can count to 10 you can do this meditation.

As you sit someplace quiet, breathing normally, count each out-breath. When you get to 10, start again at 1. If you realize that you're on 27 or that you've stopped counting altogether, start again at 1. Counting your exhalations gives your mind something tangible to focus on, which can help with the *Am I doing this right?* thoughts that so often pop up during meditation practice. To really make this practice goof-proof, set a timer for five minutes so that you don't have to wonder how much longer to keep going.

Organize Your Purse or Wallet

Think of how much stuff you cram into your wallet or purse every day. If you make this quick-and-easy chore a daily ritual when you arrive home from work, it will give you a sense of peace knowing that everything is in its place. And it will give you some built-in breathing room between the end of your workday and the start of your time at home. It takes only a few minutes to throw out the candy wrappers and receipts that you don't need. If you let this task slide, you might forget what gift card or important expense receipt you've stashed in there. You may want to create an envelope at home where you place all of your receipts to go through at a later time if it's too time consuming to do every day. Your space reflects your energy: keeping your desk, home, and even your bag clear and well-tended helps you to keep your energy tidy and calm, and helps you to let go of any energy that you pick up every day that isn't serving you.

Journal

Journaling can be a great daily habit to put your worries and stressors in perspective. It can also be a good in-the-moment release valve when you're feeling particularly upset. Writing down your issues helps you to get distance and perspective: things feel less threatening when they're written down in black and white. And journaling helps you notice any patterns in when you typically feel overwhelmed or have trouble calming down; once you spot patterns you can think about how you might react to these situations more mindfully. There's no wrong way to use your journal: you can bullet out what is bothering you, write in stream-of-consciousness, or write to someone you are having a conflict with. You can brainstorm solutions or copy down lyrics or quotes that bring you comfort in stressful times. However you choose to use your journal, remember that the practice is for you, and you don't have to worry about anyone else's judgment or commentary.

A tree that is unbending is easily broken.

—LAO TZU
Chinese philosopher and founder of Taoism

Breathe Like the Ocean

Ujjayi breath is a very calming breath that sounds like the ocean or the sound you would hear if you put your ear next to a seashell. To achieve this breath, softly draw out the word *home* as you exhale (*hhhhoooommme*). Say this word in a whisper. Now say it as you round and gently close your mouth. You can also reverse and draw in the word. It may sound like Darth Vader, only much softer and less scary.

Enjoy a Tennis Ball Massage

This exercise helps you release those knots of stress that you may be keeping in your back. Find a tennis ball that is used and just a little flat. Keep this tennis ball handy as you begin.

1. Turn on a mindless TV show, podcast, or playlist, and lie down on a rug or your yoga mat.
2. Use your right hand to place the tennis ball under your back, between your spine and your left shoulder blade.
3. Bend your left knee, placing your foot up close to your bottom.
4. Inhale, and release your hands down by your sides.
5. Exhale, and let the weight of your body slowly come down onto the tennis ball.
6. Press into your left foot to roll your back a few inches up and down over the ball. Notice the valley of knots! The tennis ball is staying on the side of the spine.
7. Find your most tender knot, and allow your body to sink over the ball. Say (or moan) *Ohhhhh.*
8. Breathe deeply. If this is too intense, put a towel between you and the tennis ball. If you want to intensify the sensation, straighten your bent leg.
9. Do the other side.

Add Meditation to Your Routine

Sitting in stillness is what meditation is all about. But it is hard to sit in stillness while our minds are chattering about all kinds of things. This happens to every one of us: this chattering mind is called Monkey Mind. Like a monkey that jumps from branch to branch, our minds can seem to jump from thought to thought. Ideally, meditation should be done every day during a time that is set aside for that reason, so you can be consistent in your practice and improve your ability to get in touch with your inner peace. Finding time for yourself every day can be very difficult for busy adults, but you can find times throughout the day to quiet your thoughts, and the possibilities are endless as far as breath and yoga postures. Pick one from this book that works best for you, and try to add it to your daily routine.

The mind is like a crazy monkey, which leaps about and never stays in one place.

—CHÖGYAM TRUNGPA RINPOCHE
Tibetan Buddhist monk and teacher

Meditate with the Mountains

Being in the mountains is a unique experience. The clear air, fresh breezes, sweeping vistas, and abundant foliage all provide nourishment for your soul. A hiking or camping trip, or even a brief day-trip into a green natural area, can help boost your inner calm. If you aren't in the mountains right now, you can visualize being there, and tap into memories of outdoor adventures for this meditation.

1. Lie down outside, if possible; if not, find a comfortable place to lie down inside. You can add small touches to remind you of the mountains, like opening a window to let the breeze in, or lighting a pine-scented candle.
2. Close your eyes.
3. Breathe long, slow breaths.
4. Let your entire body surrender into the support of the earth.
5. Picture Mother Earth wrapping her arms around you with healing love.
6. Feel the coolness of the gentle mountain breeze blow across your face and your body.
7. Stand up slowly, and take a refreshing breath, drawing in the fresh mountain air.

Take Up a New Hobby

What's a skill you've always wanted to learn? Perhaps pasta-making, dancing the tango, embroidery? Carve out ten minutes today to get started: watch a *YouTube* video, do a supply run, book a lesson, or reach out to a friend who can teach you. The combination of concentration and movement makes learning a new skill a great mind-body practice. It also short-circuits the disempowering story in your head that says, *I don't have time to do the things I want to do.* (Remember, small steps count; you don't have to master your new hobby immediately.)

Stretch in the Morning

Use the time it takes for your coffee to brew, toast to toast, or kettle to boil for this great-feeling stretch to start your day with a moment of mindful, calming self-care.

1. Place your palms on the edge of the counter and walk your feet back until your arms and spine are fully extended.
2. Bring your feet directly under your hips so your body is making the shape of an upside-down *L*. Stay here for a few breaths, feeling your spine grow a little longer with each exhale.

This is a great opener for the neck, shoulders, spine, abdomen, rib cage, and back of the legs. And it feels so good that you won't care if your family or your roommates wonder what the heck you're doing.

Admit a Mistake

Every person on earth makes mistakes regularly. Daily, even. Because every person on earth is a human, and humans aren't perfect. What most humans don't typically do regularly is admit their mistakes—too embarrassing. But here's what else not talking about your mistakes is—stressful. Keeping things hidden takes effort. And it creates fear—what if you get found out? To uncork some of this angst, make it a point to admit to a mistake in the next twenty-four hours. For example, "Here's what I wish I'd said" or "I did this thing that I feel weird about." What you confess doesn't have to be big. No matter the size of the slipup you fess up to, you'll create a noticeable release of tension. It also opens up an opportunity to feel closer to the person you tell.

Watch the Animals

Draw on the power of animals to help you find your Zen. Go to a park, where you're bound to find trees, bushes, and rocks. Take a walk through the park and walk slowly enough that you can be on the lookout for animals. Listen for sounds, stand still, and see what you can find inside trees and bushes. Bring your eyes to the ground, looking for the animals that scurry on land. When you find an animal, follow it with your eyes. What is it doing? Watch how it moves: the gentle arc of a bird's flight, or the tail twitch of a red squirrel. Breathe deeply as you watch, and take in a big breath of fresh air, smelling the scents of the outdoors—from the cut grass of your neighbor's lawn and the flowers blooming in your garden, to the spicy smell of leaves and pine needles blanketing the ground beneath the trees. Reach your energy out to the animal you are watching, and send it some love and appreciation for sharing these minutes with you. Try to keep that feeling of peace and purpose as you continue with your day.

Put Your Phone Down

As wonderful as technology is, it's also highly addictive and can keep you in a stressed-out, reactive state—*did my phone just buzz?* Take a moment to take stock of your technology use. Is there one simple change you could make that would help you be more conscious of how and when you interact with your screens? Possibilities include:

- Turn off push notifications.
- Use an old-school alarm clock instead of your phone.
- Power down all your devices at least thirty minutes before bed.
- Decide to check your email only once an hour, or at a few specific times a day.
- Decide on something you'll do before checking your phone, such as taking three breaths or doing ten jumping jacks.

Choose just one tactic you can commit to. You want to set yourself up for success—too many rules may make you feel intimidated and unmotivated.

Have patience with everyone, but especially with yourself.

—FRANCIS DE SALES
Sixteenth-century Roman Catholic saint

Visualize a Lake

Sometimes, even when you meditate, it's tricky to calm your brain down. You can quiet your body, but your thoughts dance on. Let them. If you watch your thoughts without trying to direct or interfere with them, your thoughts will slow. Here is a meditation to help you follow your thoughts rather than fight them.

1. Choose a comfortable sitting position. Support your bottom and lower back with pillows, if necessary.
2. Straighten your spine. Rest your hands, palm up, on your thighs. If you tend to feel chilly, place a soft blanket around your shoulders and over your lap. This helps you stop focusing on your body and instead turn your attention inside.
3. Close your eyes. Take a couple of cleansing breaths and then breathe in and out in a slow rhythm. Relax. Mentally let go of thoughts about your external environment. Let your heart be open and receptive.
4. Imagine your mind is a lake. Your restless thoughts are ripples pushed by a breeze blowing across the surface. When the breeze stops, the lake becomes still. Imagine the lake's surface reflecting the full moon; its light is a source of calm and well-being. Absorb the calm. Let peaceful awareness fill you completely.

Give Yourself a Bedtime Massage

If you have trouble falling asleep or need a bit of extra help to settle yourself down after a stressful day, give yourself a massage before going to bed. First heat some oil for massaging until it's warm to the touch. You can use sesame oil, coconut oil, or anything you have on hand that's good for your skin. Then with slow, soothing strokes, massage your feet with the warm oil. Wash your hands and cover your feet with socks so you don't stain your bedsheets with oil. Massage warm oil along your brow line and at the crown of your head as you take deep, soothing breaths.

Take a Cheap Flight on a Whim

Feeling like you need to change things up a little and add some spontaneity to your life? Are you stuck in a stress rut and just need to get away? Check your preferred airline's website and see what the cheapest flight is for the upcoming weekend. Maybe it's only a two- or three-day getaway, but leaving the day-to-day monotony behind and taking an exciting last-minute trip will remind you why you work those long hours in the first place. Taking some time away can help you put your life back into perspective and help remind you of what's important in life. The spontaneity of the trip will also lessen the stress leading up to the getaway. It's said that the best time to purchase inexpensive airline tickets is Wednesday evening. See what you can find!

Take a Tai Chi Class

Tai chi is a martial art that has been practiced for centuries. Created in China, it's a slow practice that promotes health and reduces stress. Using flowing movements and steady breathing, tai chi has been known to lower blood pressure, increase circulation and flexibility, and is perfect for people who have limited mobility. Find a gym or martial arts studio that offers classes and take one today. You'll enjoy the graceful movements and feel an overall sense of well-being.

Set peace of mind as your highest goal, and organize your life around it.

—BRIAN TRACY
Canadian-American motivational speaker and author

Move to Music

Music is a great way to shift your energy and let go of stress. Just find your favorite low-key artist or album, and turn it on. There isn't a right or wrong way to dance: let the music be your body's guide. If you aren't used to dancing or letting the music inform your movement, try this:

When you turn on the music, close your eyes and pause. Wait a few moments to let the rhythm of the beat and the sounds affect your body; you don't have to think about it. After several moments, allow yourself to move in any way you like. You can sway, rock, or perform a few dance steps if you know any. You can wrap your arms around yourself and give yourself a comforting hug, or reach up to the sky and stretch. You can hum or sing along. The body knows what it needs; it will inform you. Move with a light attitude— no one is judging you. Smile as your body flows through space, and allow your mood to shift toward calm.

Breathe Away Your Anxiety

Breathing effectively is one of the easiest ways to uplift your energy and calm yourself down quickly. If taking a deep breath is difficult for you, consider softening your body. You can do this in a number of places. First relax the muscles in your face, the corners of your mouth, your shoulders, and your upper back. Then sit up tall and relax your shoulder blades. Notice if you pulled down the tops of your shoulders to do this. If you did, try this method of relaxing your shoulders instead: Imagine that your shoulder blades rest on your back like wings. You can activate your wings by squeezing them toward one another (around the back of your heart). Squeeze them together and release a few times. Notice how this gently encourages your shoulders to relax while it simultaneously loosens your jaw. Movements such as this help you get out of your head and into your body. Remember to focus on your breathing. If focusing on your abdomen while you breathe is discouraging, try shifting your awareness to the sides of your waist or even your lower back and breathe deeply into those areas. Release the need to do things perfectly or right.

Look for the Light Around You

You may have heard the word *namaste* at your yoga class or seen it on a T-shirt. The translation for this Sanskrit phrase of greeting is something like "I bow to the Divine in you" or "the light in me sees the light in you." This phrase acknowledges that the world is made of goodness and light; it's important to remember this, especially when you are feeling anxious, stressed, or worried. You can recognize and take comfort in the light and energy that come from the people and things that are all around you. Saying *namaste* in greeting is a gentle way to bless the world and all its beings.

If we learn to
open our hearts,
anyone, including
the people who
drive us crazy,
can be our teacher.

—PEMA CHÖDRÖN
American Buddhist nun, teacher, and author

Move with Purpose

Physical exercise can do wonders for your peace of mind, as well as your physical health. Sometimes you can even heal minor discomforts through exercise. The American Heart Association says we should get at least 150 minutes per week of moderate exercise or seventy-five minutes per week of vigorous exercise (or a combination of the two types of activity). Thirty minutes a day, five times a week, is an easy goal to remember. This cardio can be done in an endless number of ways, depending on what kind of movement brings you the most joy. Walking, dancing, biking, running, yoga, rock climbing, and weight lifting are all popular ways to get your heart pumping. You can be mindful of your movement at other times outside your workout as well: simple changes such as parking your car farther away from the store or taking the stairs instead of the elevator can boost your heart rate. If you need support for getting motivated, you might consider joining a walking group, hiring a personal trainer, or joining a specialty gym or class to learn skills like martial arts or dance. Be sure to incorporate some stretching and strength training into your routine. Do what it takes to make movement count today.

Do Cat-Cow

Cat Pose and Cow Pose are two yoga exercises that help to stretch out and engage your back and shoulders, and can help you shrug off stress when you're feeling overwhelmed. The poses work even better when combined into a flow. Here's how it's done:

1. Get on your hands and knees on your yoga mat or a soft blanket. Keep your shoulders above your hands, and your hips above your knees; this is called Tabletop Pose.
2. Shift into Cow Pose: lift your chest and your bottom and let your belly drop, creating a gentle arch to your back.
3. Shift into Cat Pose: lift your stomach and tuck your tailbone, and tuck your chin to your chest, rounding your back like a stretching cat. Repeat this back-and-forth flow gently until you feel better.

You can do this little flow just about anywhere: try a modified version in your desk chair or in the car. Just alternate between Cow Pose with your tailbone up and your shoulders back with your chest up, and Cat Pose, where you curl in your tailbone and round your spine. This flow is very helpful in opening up your heart chakra, which can help move stuck emotional energy and allow you to be more receptive to compassion and love.

Imagine a Shield of Golden Light

This visualization is a powerful energetic defense against stress and negative energy. You can use it whenever you feel overwhelmed and need to create your own peace.

1. Repeat the mantra, *I am protected by the golden light that surrounds me now.*
2. As you speak the words, imagine golden light shining out of you, creating a protective shield around your body.
3. Visualize bad energy bouncing off your "shield" and away, and your bright light shining against the darkness of a bad mood—yours or someone else's.

The more you practice this visualization, the better it works at repelling negativity and creating space for calm and peace.

Exhale Stress, Inhale Calm

Let's get this straight: not all stress is bad. In fact, stress is a normal, natural, and necessary part of life. But if your thoughts are predominately stressful in nature, or you find you are no longer enjoying life due to excessive thinking and pressure, then consider reciting this mantra: *I breathe in peace, I breathe out excess stress.* Allow it to shift you gently back to your most natural state of balance and ease. Be sure to breathe as you state this mantra to yourself out loud. See your breath as beautiful colors (yellows, blues, and greens) gently moving in and out of your body.

✦

The greatest
weapon against
stress is our
ability to choose
one thought
over another.

—WILLIAM JAMES
American psychologist and philosopher

Take the Pressure Off

Putting timelines in your life may help you stay on task. However, if you find you are feeling pressured by having to achieve something in a certain order or by a certain deadline, remind yourself that you are enough, just as you are. Your accomplishments may very well be something to strive for, but they by no means measure your worth. You already have everything you need. Setting goals and pursuing your dreams expand who you already are rather than who you hope or wish to be.

Narrow Your Focus

You can perform this exercise at any point during the day when you have a moment to yourself. Narrowing your focus on one thing can help you block out distractions so you can solve an issue or problem, or it can simply bring you back to the here and now if you ever get stuck in your head. You can make great progress in any undertaking you choose if you have the ability to focus diligently on the task at hand.

1. Choose one thing to concentrate on. It can be your breathing, the color of your curtains, the smell of a candle, an image in your head, or the sound of rain beating against the windows.
2. Whenever you find your attention wandering, bring it back to your point of concentration. Do this without judgment: you can think to yourself *come on back* if it helps to pull your focus back to your original subject.
3. Your concentration should be firm but not forced. The more you practice this exercise, the easier it will become.
4. While performing this exercise, breathe deeply and regularly. If this is your point of concentration, time the breathing—one beat in, two beats out—and maintain this pattern.

When you're ready to end your practice (either when your timer goes off, or you feel relaxed and ready to get back to your day), you can start slowly expanding your attention to bring in more of your senses.

Carry a Sacred Souvenir

Whenever you find yourself in a sacred place—anywhere you find peace and inspiration, from a church or temple to the ocean and the mountains—bring home little keepsakes that are small enough to carry on your person, either in your pocket or purse or on a bracelet or necklace. Hold this amulet in your hand or place it on your heart or the third-eye space on your forehead whenever you need to call on it for extra protection and guidance. If you're feeling overwhelmed and want a moment of peace, pull out your souvenir and spend some time with it. Examine the texture, and look at the pattern or text of your object. Feel its rough edges or smooth surface. Rub the object gently between your fingers. Is it cold? Warm from your pocket? Try to remember the feeling you had when you got your souvenir, and bring that feeling of peace or meditation back to you right now.

✦

Your sacred
space is where
you can find
yourself again
and again.

—JOSEPH CAMPBELL
American professor and author

Shout It Out

Being calm and mindful doesn't mean you won't ever get angry or upset again. But it can help you express those emotions in a more conscious way. If you've got some anger to express, let it out with a primal scream (preferably somewhere solitary where you won't scare anyone else, like in the car). Do it with the intention of getting the feelings out of your body and into the air where they can dissipate. This exercise gives your frustrations a voice, making it less likely that you'll end up yelling when it comes time to discuss whatever's upsetting you. As a result you'll be more likely to be heard.

Tidy Up

Clutter suppresses and even obstructs energy flow. Stagnant or blocked energy makes your life difficult, and can make you anxious. Sapped of energy, your health suffers. Stagnant energy also blocks the flow of money, impedes the manifestation of healthy relationships, obstructs advancements in your chosen career path, and can bring on depression and negative patterns of thought. The condition of your physical space reflects what's going on in your mind. Taking the time to tidy your space helps you to tidy, organize, and soothe your mind.

To start, pick a particular room or area of your home or office to organize. Tidy it, throwing away things you no longer use or need. If you haven't touched something in six months, chances are you don't need it. Once that area is completed, tackle the next room and the next until the whole house or area is re-energized. Use baskets (symbolizing the reeds and grasses of nature) with lids to organize objects in a room that were carried in and forgotten. Left to pile up, clutter begins to slow down or block a space's natural flow of energy.

Stop and Listen

Nature is filled with sounds of peace. The sound of water trickling outside of your window, birds chirping, or the breeze blowing gently through the trees can soothe your nervous system. Take time to listen and notice these sounds in your daily life. If these peaceful sounds get disrupted, as they sometimes do (by things like leaf blowers or children crying), learn to develop your ability to notice what is near and far. Sure, the leaf blower might be loud and disruptive, but remember the closest sound you have is the sound of your breath. Withdraw (e.g., close the window) from distractions the best you can and return to your breath.

✦

How can you ever know anything if you are too busy thinking?

—GAUTAMA BUDDHA

Sixth-century spiritual leader and founder of Buddhism

Try Alternate Nostril Breathing

Alternate nostril breathing is a wonderful breathing technique for producing a calm and steady breath pattern. To do this, breathe in through one nostril, and exhale out the other. Then inhale through that side, and exhale out the first.

1. Sit comfortably with the spine straight.
2. Hold your right hand with your pointer and second finger bent against your palm and your other fingers extended; this is called the Vishnu mudra.
3. Close off the right nostril with the right thumb.
4. Softly breathe in through the left nostril.
5. At the top of that breath, close off the left nostril with the right ring finger and exhale through the right nostril.
6. At the bottom of that exhale, breathe back in through the right nostril.
7. At the top of that inhale, close off the right nostril with the right thumb and exhale out the left nostril.
8. Repeat this pattern for a minute or two, keeping the breath soft, regular, and steady, and the shoulders relaxed.

Make Peaceful Breathing a Practice

A practice is something you choose to repeat daily. Think about it: if you wanted to get good at playing the piano, then you would most likely practice it on a daily basis. The same goes for writing, reading, or playing a sport. Developing peace in your daily life is no different. The more you practice breathing, the better you get at it. Only instead of learning how to breathe faster, you will breathe deeply and slowly with conscious awareness. Make time every day to focus on your breath; you can try a breathing exercise from this book (like alternate nostril breathing or Ujjayi breath), or you can simply notice your breath, paying attention to the quality and depth of your breathing without trying to change it.

Be Grateful for Yourself

Being you means you are able to allow your own thoughts, feelings, and beliefs to emerge with honor and respect. This does not mean you have to act on every little thing. Notice if you start to compare yourself to others or question your abilities and strengths. Take these doubts as a sign that you may be veering away from your sense of being. Your path is always being shaped by the way you respond to what is happening inside of you. To get back on your course, put your attention on the now, and take time to pause and appreciate all the great things that make you who you are. You can jot them down on a notepad or just list them in your head. Take time to reflect on each item, and tell yourself *thank you for being you*.

♦

I love people.
I love my family,
my children...but
inside myself is a
place where I live
all alone and that's
where you renew
your springs that
never dry up.

—PEARL S. BUCK
American author

Hydrate

Sometimes one of the most helpful things you can do for your body when you're feeling anxious or stressed is to have a drink of water. Human bodies are about two-thirds water, but many people are mildly dehydrated and don't know it. While severe dehydration has dramatic symptoms and can even result in death, mild dehydration may go unnoticed and is more likely to occur after intense exercise, in extreme heat, while dieting, and when you've been physically ill, either from illness or as a result of food poisoning or drinking too much alcohol. Taking good care of your body can help you feel better and make you more resilient to stress, and it can also help remind you that you are important and deserve love and care.

Repeat This Prayer from
the Cheyenne People

Although separated by vast regions of geography and climate, many Native American peoples share the belief that the creative spirit can be accessed through nature. The key to achieving that is experiencing and living in harmony with natural forces. There are many ways to pursue this goal by carefully observing animals, weather patterns, and the elements of wind, sun, and moon. Many Native Americans believe that the spirit of the observed can communicate with human beings and enlarge their understanding. These efforts are not seen as tasks or methods to be learned. Rather they are viewed as extended meditations, or living meditatively. On the following page is a Cheyenne prayer that you can say to yourself to gain a quiet moment of inspiration:

Let us know peace.

For as long as the
moon shall rise,

For as long as rivers
shall flow,

For as long as the
sun shall shine,

For as long as the
grass shall grow,

Let us know peace.

Do a Metta Meditation

When you focus on loving-kindness toward yourself and others, anxiety and fear will no longer dominate your feelings. Going through life with such an appreciation encourages generosity, compassion, and a feeling of peace. This practice is called *metta meditation*, in which you concentrate your energy on sending compassion to yourself and to other people.

1. Close your eyes; draw your attention inward to your heart center. Picture your tender heart, and say to yourself: *May I be brave and wise and happy.* Repeat this a few times in your mind.
2. Next, think of someone you love whose courage and compassion you admire. Picture that person in your mind, and repeat this thought: *May you be brave and wise and happy.*
3. Then picture someone you find challenging or difficult, and address this person in the same way: *May you be brave and wise and happy.*
4. Next, broaden your statement to include everyone: *May all beings be brave and wise and happy.*
5. Finally, come back to yourself. Again picture your tender heart, and say to yourself: *May I be brave and wise and happy.* Repeat this a few times in your mind.

Practice this exercise whenever you feel overwhelmed by fear or anxiety; it helps quiet your mind by gently reminding you of the deep ties that connect all beings.

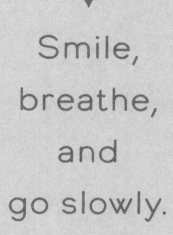

Smile,
breathe,
and
go slowly.

—THICH NHAT HANH
Buddhist monk and author

Do Cobbler's Pose

A great yoga position for relaxation is called Cobbler's Pose. This pose gets its name from the position that cobblers in India traditionally assumed while they worked. Designed to open the hips and release tension, Cobbler's Pose is a wonderful way to unwind. You can do it anytime, but it's especially effective when done in bed at the end of the day.

1. To begin, lie on your back in bed.
2. Bend your knees, bringing your feet closer to your hips, and then open your knees to the sides. To make the pose more comfortable, you can put a pillow under each knee.
3. You can read a book while in this pose (make sure you have sufficient reading light), or just hold the pose for a few minutes in the dark before you fall asleep.

Lie Out under the Stars

Sometimes all it takes is lying down in the grass and looking up at the infinite sky above to remind you that we are a small piece of this incredible universe. It's extremely beneficial to take time to appreciate the beauty and vastness of what lies beyond us; it puts our daily stress into perspective. Looking up at the night sky will help relax your mind and inspire you to do big things! Make sure to turn off those backyard sensor lights that will go off with a passing wind, and take a blanket so you can get comfortable.

Center Yourself

The best way to find your inner peace often involves centering yourself. It also allows you to carve out a moment of tranquility in an otherwise hectic day. This is a good exercise to do before more rigorous yoga poses or other physical activity, since it helps to enliven the mind-body connection.

1. Sit in a comfortable, seated position with your legs crossed.
2. Place a cushion or a folded blanket under your bottom; this helps you sit up tall while maintaining the natural curves in your spine.
3. Gently place your hands in your lap. Close your eyes. Relax your forehead, eyes, jaw, and tongue.
4. Scan all the way down your body, relaxing each body part as you breathe in and out naturally.
5. After scanning the body, simply watch the breath as it flows in and out. Do this for a few breaths.
6. Begin breathing deeply. Allow the belly, ribs, and chest to expand in three dimensions as you inhale. As you exhale, allow the chest, ribs, and belly to relax.
7. Continue breathing deep, filling breaths for several breaths. Then return to the natural breath, and open your eyes.

Who among
us has the
extra time to
not live every
moment fully?

—JUDITH HANSON LASATER
American yoga teacher

Have an Acupuncture Treatment

Acupuncture is an ancient Chinese medical treatment that has been practiced for centuries. It involves inserting and manipulating small, thin needles into different areas of the body for the purpose of relieving pain and stress. The areas of the body where the needles are placed follow the meridians where vital life-force energy (also called *qi* or *chi*) flows. People get acupuncture for a variety of health reasons. Find an acupuncturist in your area to get a treatment. Let them know where your pain is and what you would like to accomplish with acupuncture. Do some research before your first visit so you know a little about what to expect and can ask questions.

Hand-Wash Your Dishes

Doing chores mindfully can be a sort of meditation, especially after a long day. It can feel good to focus fully on a manual task, especially one that benefits you and your household.

Washing dishes is a perfect example of a chore that can be done mindfully. Fill the sink with soapy water (try to be a mindful shopper and buy products that are beautifully scented and perhaps organic). When you plunge your hands into the soapy water, enjoy the sensation of warmth. Then wash each glass and dish slowly, surrendering any desire to rush the process or to focus on getting them all done. Rather, focus on just one item at a time. Appreciate your dishware as you line up each item carefully in the dish rack to air-dry.

Do a Forward Fold

If your day is not going well, and you feel yourself moments away from blowing a gasket, you need a time-out to calm down. Forward-bending postures will calm the nervous system. Try this short, simple exercise.

1. Stand with your feet hip-width apart, with toes facing forward. Bring your arms to your sides.
2. Allow your tailbone to reach downward, and lengthen your spine upward. Press out through the crown of your head. Soften your knees so they are slightly bent.
3. Reach your arms up above your head, inhale, and as you exhale, fold over to touch your toes or reach close to them. Hang like a rag doll. Your head should not have any tension.
4. Stay for a few breaths. You can sway back and forth, sweeping your fingertips side to side. Gently nod *yes*, then gently shake your head *no*.
5. Come up slowly, rolling one vertebra over the other like you are stacking coins. Your head should come up last. You can do this as many times as you'd like, to feel calm and refreshed.

✦

Everything we
do is infused
with the energy
with which we do it.
If we're frantic,
life will be frantic.
If we're peaceful,
life will be peaceful.

—MARIANNE WILLIAMSON
Spiritual teacher, author, and lecturer

Figure Out What Sets You Off

Stress is universal, but it's also personal—what sends one person into a spiral will float right by someone else. What types of situations make your stress meter spike? Traffic? Coming home to a messy house? Being criticized? Take time today to pay attention to the things that set you off. You may be able to notice a pattern that you can then go about changing. Also, it's a scientific fact that the simple act of observing a process can modify its outcome.

Chant *Lam*

When you find yourself in crisis mode, your fight-or-flight response kicks in, which is a direct challenge to your first chakra, the root chakra. This chakra, located at the base of the spine, relates to our connection to the earth; it's the seat of the survival instinct. When overcome by anxiety, your mind spins in circles of worry, your heart beats faster, your breath becomes shallow, and your belly becomes upset. When you are anxious, your energy is predominantly up in your mind. A great way to ground your energy when you find yourself in this state is to chant the sound that is traditionally connected to the root chakra, which is *lam*. If the weather permits, get outside to allow the earth's force to help ground you. Whether or not you can get outside, breathe in slowly, feeling your body expand to allow the air to rush inward on the inhale. Envision your connection to the earth as you imagine your inhale going through your body into the ground. On the exhale, chant the sound *lam*. Create a longer exhalation than inhalation to induce relaxation. Feel the vibration of the word as you speak it: see if you can feel it vibrate through your body before sinking into the earth. See if you can feel your connection to the earth through your feet. This exercise should leave you feeling solid and grounded.

♦

Oh soul,

You worry too much.

You have seen your own strength.

You have seen your own beauty.

You have seen your golden wings.

Of anything less,

Why do you worry?

You are in truth

The soul, of the soul, of the soul.

—RUMI
Thirteenth-century Persian philosopher, theologian, and poet

Sleep on Luxurious Sheets

We spend one-third of our lives in bed sleeping. Don't you want that bed to be as comfortable as possible? A good night's sleep can help you have a more peaceful morning and a productive day. Sure, sheets can be expensive, but you don't need to buy them that often, so make the investment; you're worth it. Take a trip to your favorite department store and splurge on a high thread count. The higher the thread count the softer the sheets will feel, and that's always a good thing. If you're worried about the cost, try looking at a discount store; some chains often carry a wide variety of expensive bedding items at lower prices.

Put Your Feet Up

Hop into bed and swing your legs up, resting them gently against the headboard (or wall). Squiggle closer until your bottom is as close as is comfortably possible to the headboard. Have your arms by your sides, palms facing up. Lift your hips by bending your knees and pressing your feet onto the headboard. When you lift your hips, slide a pillow under your lower back and the top of your hips to lift them up, so your tailbone curls over the pillow. You want to have a gentle lift of your hips that also allows your lower back to tilt toward the mattress. Your back should feel as if it is arched naturally, and not a strong arch. Then straighten your legs, and stay in this position, allowing the blood to rush out of your feet, legs, and hips, giving your heart a rest. This pose will relieve tired legs and mild backaches, as well as provide a gentle stretch for the backs of your legs. It's also the perfect time to breathe in and out, focusing your mind on the renewing energy that comes with breath, and then noticing the calm and relaxation that result from quieting the mind and being attentive to your breath. Breathe in peace; breathe out frustration. Stay in this position for ten to fifteen minutes while you practice long, slow breaths. This is also a nice pose in which to practice gratitude by saying a prayer of thanksgiving. If you can truly feel thankful even for a bad day, you will be on your way to enjoying a sound sleep.

Wrap Yourself in a Rainbow Light

Rainbows can represent peace, comfort, insight, and life after death. They are one of the few occurrences in life that get you to stop and look up at the sky. Rainbows are also a wonderful way to shield and protect yourself and others from negative influences. Visualize a rainbow light wrapped around you for miles like bubble wrap, keeping you safe and warm. Be sure to add a little extra white, gold, and silver shimmer look to your rainbow. While you create this visualization, strengthen it with an affirmative statement, such as *I clear and shield my energy with this beautiful rainbow light*. If you do this practice and recite this mantra before bed, it will help you have a good night's sleep. But this is also a great exercise to do any time you feel unsettled to help you feel more secure.

◆

Nothing can bring you peace but yourself.

—RALPH WALDO EMERSON
American poet and author

Perform the Simplest Meditation

Meditation is about focusing your mind and concentrating on your breath. You can meditate anywhere at any time, especially if you keep it simple. Try this simple meditation to calm your mind when you're feeling stressed. All you have to do is follow the breath and anchor it to a word or phrase.

1. Inhale and say silently to yourself *Peace*.
2. Exhale and say silently to yourself *Relax*.

Inhale...*Peace*. Exhale...*Relax*. Have no agenda—just the breath. This seems almost too simple, but the results can be significant in terms of releasing stress, slowing down, and centering yourself.

Look Away from the Screen

Staring at a screen all day makes your physical world seem small; it also tires your eyes, and an unbreaking focus on work can keep you stressed and anxious. Taking a break to look at something different will shift your perspective and your vision, and give you a short break. Spend the next few minutes looking at something far away—a painting across the room, perhaps, or the view out a window. It will help you remember that there's more going on in the world than whatever is 2 feet in front of you.

Stop Worrying about Other People

Worrying about someone you love disempowers them and puts your focus on what could go wrong instead of what's going right. This is not very helpful, and it can keep you stressed out. Here's a way to support someone from afar that's good for them and for you. It's a loving-kindness meditation, and it goes like this:

Sitting up tall, close your eyes and call up an image of this person in your mind. Really "see" them as you silently repeat, as many times as feels good: *May you be happy. May you be free from suffering. May you be at peace.*

Then do your best to let go of your worry.

✦

There are two
ways of meeting
difficulties: you alter
the difficulties or
you alter yourself
meeting them.

—PHYLLIS BOTTOME
English author

Put Fresh Flowers in Your House

You can evoke the soothing essence of nature simply by filling a vase with flowers and placing it in any room in the house. Notice how just the presence of a living thing or the sweet scent of freshly cut blooms can change the energy of the space—and your energy along with it. Choose blooms in your favorite color, or with the most vibrant scent. Selecting your flowers can be a meditative action as well: take your time to look at the petals of each flower, and take in the different smells.

Steam Away Stress with Essential Oils

Especially at certain times of year or in climates where the air is dry, steaming with an essential oil is a fast way to get the benefits of the oil. The vapor infused with healing properties rises into the nasal passages, entering your system immediately. Steaming is an effective, easy, and soothing way to explore various essential oils. To maximize the calming effect, try soothing oils like lavender, chamomile, or ylang ylang.

1. Have a towel and your essential oil nearby.
2. Get a bowl that is approximately 10 to 12 inches in diameter.
3. Boil enough water to fill the bowl one-half to two-thirds full.
4. Pour the steaming water into the bowl, and then add one drop of the essential oil to the bowl.
5. Lean your head into the flow of the steam, and put the towel over your head to cover your head and the bowl.
6. Inhale deeply through both nostrils, exhale gently through the mouth. Repeat this several times.
7. If you would like to, also close one nostril with your finger, and inhale and exhale through one nostril at a time to make sure that each side is receiving the benefits.
8. If one drop of the essential oil wasn't strong enough, or if the scent diminishes, add another drop. It's doubtful you will need more than two drops of the essential oil.
9. When you're finished steaming, sit down. Take a moment to notice the effects. Practice this two or three times a day if you're working with a particular imbalance or onset of a cold.

Learning to let go should be learned before learning to get. Life should be touched, not strangled. You've got to relax, let it happen at times, and at others move forward with it.

—RAY BRADBURY
American author

Eat Lunch Outside

Getting out of the office for a lunch break is one of the most important things to do during the day. You need to get away to recharge your battery and refocus, even if it's just for a thirty-minute lunch break. The quickest way to get some relaxation is to find a park that is close to work, or even just a picnic table nearby, and have a picnic for yourself. Before you leave for work in the morning, or even the night before, pack a picnic basket with a lunch you can look forward to all day. A grilled chicken salad with baby spinach, strawberries, and blueberries is not only delicious, but offers protein and important antioxidants. Remember to pack some healthy snacks that will give you a boost during the last half of the day; bring tangerines or clementines for a quick burst of energy and some toasted almonds or cashews for long-lasting energy. Don't forget to add something a little decadent like a chocolate cupcake or a few oatmeal raisin cookies. Sit in the sun and close your eyes. Forget what you have to do when you get back to work; just enjoy your time away from the office. This is something you can do every day to treat yourself right.

Gather Seashells

Collecting seashells is a classic beachside hobby. The activity of picking up and appreciating the shells is very soothing, and it provides you with a souvenir to remind you of the peaceful, rejuvenating effect of the ocean. Grab a big bucket and go for a long walk on the shore. You will find many varieties of shells, like iridescent mussel shells and scallop shells. You might even find some other treasures: starfish, driftwood, sea glass, and stones that the waves and sand have polished. You can use the shells that you find as decoration in your house. Pile them onto a plate and place a large pillar candle in the middle that reminds you of the ocean. Or just keep them in a special box and add to them every year. These natural mementos will make you feel like digging your toes in the warm sand, even in the middle of winter.

✦

A quiet
mind
cureth all.

—ROBERT BURTON
Seventeenth-century English scholar

Treat Yourself

You can help take your stress level down a notch and realign your equilibrium by taking some time to treat and pamper yourself with whatever makes you feel good. Go see a movie you've been interested in, or visit your favorite day-trip destination. You can go to the salon or spa, or get a massage or other treatment. How about a game of golf in the middle of the afternoon on a weekday? (So you'll have the course to yourself!) You can even treat yourself with some special at-home downtime: a few hours curled up with a good book; an extra-long, steamy shower; or hitting the sack decadently early can feel so, so good!

◆

Chaotic people often have chaotic lives, and I think they create that. But if you try and have an inner peace and a positive attitude, I think you attract that.

—IMELDA STAUNTON
English actress

Feel Your Breath

If you're feeling super stressed, this meditative breathing exercise that's doable anywhere can be a quick fix. Sit (or lie down), rest your hand on your belly, and feel your breath. As you breathe in, your belly will rise, and as you breathe out, it will fall. Follow your breath for a while. Then start to breathe at this rhythm: count to five on the inhale and count to five on the exhale. Breathe however is most comfortable for you. If you want to make this exercise even more powerful, you can breathe in through your nose and out through your mouth. If you'd like, make the exhale audible with an *ahh*. Do this for a few minutes, and notice how the simple act of breathing can calm your emotions.

Spend a Day in Bed

Ever have a morning when you wake up before work and just want to lie in bed all day? Why not actually do it, just once? Take a day off from work and don't leave bed for the *whole* day. If need be, grab your laptop and work from the comfort of your pillows and duvet. And if taking a day off isn't going to be possible any time soon, then on Saturday or Sunday when you should be taking care of the weekend chores, enjoy your meals and a few good movies from your sleeping sanctuary. Although you may get restless and want to get up and clean those dirty dishes, fight the temptation and try to allow your body to relax and enjoy some R&R. If you have to, use a Do Not Disturb sign on the door to keep out any unwanted guests.

Color

As a kid you probably spent hours coloring with markers, crayons, and colored pencils. Remember trying really hard to stay inside the lines? Now that you're a grownup, you can relax and not worry so much about boundaries. Creative activity is a great way to calm your mind and focus your energy. So go out and buy your favorite coloring tools, and since this pastime has become popular with people of all ages, you'll find plenty of coloring books made for adults. Spend the afternoon coloring away; doing it while sprawled out on the living room floor, the way you did when you were little, is always an option.

✦

The affairs of
the world will
go on forever.
Do not delay
the practice
of meditation.

—MILAREPA
Eleventh-century Tibetan yogi and poet

Find Your Breathing Space

Where is your breathing space? Where do you feel most at ease? What time of day is most peaceful to you? Think about where and when you can take a minute, away from all distractions, and breathe. If you don't have a designated space already, look for one that you can start training your brain to associate with calm. Consider taking a moment to roam outside. Be curious about the breathing spaces around you. Perhaps you'll notice a tree, your front porch step, or a certain pathway. A breathing space can also be a special area in your home where you can limit distractions (like television noise, phone alerts, new emails, or interruptions from family members). Such a space might be a quiet corner of your bedroom, a path outside, a certain chair or spot at the kitchen table where you see the birds clearly through a window, or anywhere else you can go to find a moment to breathe. Make time to spend at least a few minutes in your breathing space every day.

Be a River of Peace

Rivers tend to run from higher altitudes to lower altitudes. Gravity causes the water to flow down peaks and valleys, with some water seeping deep into the ground while the remainder rolls off. Being a river of peace is similar. Peace is a higher-vibrational sensation that comes across time and space, trickling down into lower-dimensional frequencies such as the human body. Picture this river in your head, and say to yourself, *I am a river of peace.* Breathe in and out as you repeat this phrase, feeling the sensation of calm spread and flow through you.

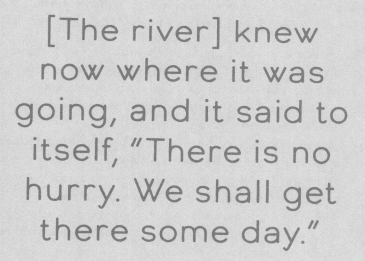

[The river] knew now where it was going, and it said to itself, "There is no hurry. We shall get there some day."

—A.A. MILNE
English author

Use Mala Beads to Meditate

You can help focus your mind by using *malas* during your meditation. Malas are beads, strung on a loop, numbering 108. This is a sacred number in the yogic tradition. Mala beads are made of various materials, including wood, gemstones, and crystals. As you infuse them with blessings and prayers, your malas will hold that vibration. This kind of repeated mantra meditation is called *japa*.

1. Get in a comfortable position for meditation, in a quiet spot.
2. Choose a mantra. This can be any phrase that has power for you. The most basic mantra is *Om*, but you can use the similar-sounding word *Calm* or another word or phrase that symbolizes calming energy to you.
3. Start with the bead next to the "guru" bead, which is the bead at the knot. Hold the first bead between your thumb and middle finger. Move the beads between those two fingers, one by one; at each bead repeat the mantra you've chosen.
4. When you've passed each bead through your fingers and you arrive at the guru bead, you've done 108 repetitions of the mantra. Do not cross over or use the guru bead. Instead, you can do another round by passing the beads between your fingers in the other direction.
5. After you've completed your meditation for the number of rounds you've chosen, take a few moments to stop and integrate the experience. Allow the effects of the japa to resonate within you.

Enjoy Some Art

We are subjected every day to thousands, if not millions, of visual images: on billboards, on our cell phones, on websites, and on fliers delivered to our mailbox. The sheer number means that useless images can crowd out those that can be helpful. The solution? Take a moment to meditate on something truly lovely.

1. Select a piece of art. This could be a drawing, a painting, or a photograph; or a sculpture or the architecture of a building. You can choose a famous piece of art or something you created yourself; just be sure that it's something you consider really lovely, and that brings you joy. Place it (or yourself) where you can see all the details.
2. Focus your attention on the artwork. Take your time looking at its color. Notice how the light around it affects the shade, shadow, and depth of the color.
3. Now close your eyes and see those same details. Take your time to evoke in your mind all that you saw with your eyes opened.
4. Open your eyes to see if the visual image is the same as the mental image. If you notice a difference, do the exercise once more.

Be Late for Work

Call or email your boss this morning and say you'll be a little late. Use that bit of extra time to do something nice for yourself. Make a delicious breakfast, do some yoga, have sex, or take the dog for a longer walk. Sometimes it can seem like we're always rushing around, so this morning take all the time you need. You won't be stuck in traffic on your way to work, and chances are you'll have a much more pleasant, less stressful day.

✦

When instead of reacting against a situation, you merge with it, the solution arises out of the situation itself.

—ECKHART TOLLE
German-born spiritual teacher and author

Repeat a Mantra

Repeating a mantra can be a very effective way to stop stressful thoughts and redirect your brain toward peace and calm. You can use any phrase you like: a song lyric, a poem, or a phrase you write yourself for a specific goal or purpose. Writing your own mantra might sound appealing, but it's trickier than you think. The key is to center yourself through breathing and connecting to the present moment before jotting down ideas. To be effective, mantras should be written as if the intended situation is already happening. For this reason, you should use present-tense language. One of the most powerful mantras you can write and state is *I am*. It is easy to get caught up in wanting your mantra to sound flowery, or in trying to make it rhyme perfectly. Avoid those temptations and instead focus on communicating with the universe as well as your subconscious mind. Focus on what you want to create, rather than on rhymes or adjectives. Once you choose a mantra, repeat it to yourself when you have a moment of quiet in your day. It's best to repeat it multiple times; there is power in odd numbers, so be sure to repeat your mantra an odd number of times every time you use it.

Lift Your Face to the Sun

Think about how good you feel after sitting (even briefly) in the sun. Not only does the sun give you vitamin D, which is essential to maintaining a positive mood and healthy bones, it also strengthens the energy field around you (also known as your aura), helping you to become more resilient to stress and negative energy. If you work or live in a high-pressure or negative environment, consider taking time to go outside for a few minutes a day (particularly if it's sunny). When you do, take a moment to express gratitude to the sun for providing you with light and warmth, and for sharing its energy with you.

Hit Pause

Everyday life continually poses challenges to our inner peace. In the midst of a stressful episode, whether at home or at work, we often long for the peaceful moments that a secluded, quiet meditation offers. But the real world doesn't offer such moments when they're most needed; you have to create them. At these times, a conscious pause can refresh your body and mind just as well as an extended meditation session. Just stop and take action—or no action, as the case may be.

1. If you find yourself particularly stressed, feeling that you've come to the end of your rope, stop. Remind yourself that this is an opportune time for momentary meditation, to refresh and relax your mind.
2. Pause all thoughts and remind yourself that your inner peace prevails at this moment. Think of that peace as a place within you. Straighten your spine as you do this, and lift your chin upward. Focus your eyes above your head, at the ceiling or wall.
3. Take a conscious breath, slowly and deliberately. Think of your place of peace opening its door as the air fills your lungs. On exhaling, appreciate the moment for allowing you to pause, and then return to the work at hand.

Within you there is a stillness and sanctuary to which you can retreat any time and be yourself.

—HERMANN HESSE
German poet and author

Challenge Your Body

Athletes frequently talk about being "in the zone"—the mental freedom they experience when the body is completely involved in meeting a challenge, such as running a long distance or climbing a steep incline. The focus required to perform vigorous physical labor, such as carrying heavy loads with great care or chopping wood, can also bring uncommon mind-body awareness. Working with your body can be a great way to fight stress, since it gets you out of your head and focused on the exertion. You can pursue your own "zone" by trying a challenging exercise: for you that might be a brisk hike, a weight-lifting session at the gym, or even something like pushing your heavy mower across the lawn. If it makes you sweat, you're on the right track.

Take a Bath

A bath is a classic remedy for stress, especially if you enjoy it mindfully. Turn off your overhead lights and light a few candles. Add fragrant bath oil or bath salts to the water, and play soft, soothing music, if you like.

1. Once you're in the water, take a few deep breaths and exhale with a soothing *Ahhhhhhh*. Notice how light your body feels when submerged in the water.
2. Imagine the water washing away the stresses of the moment so you can emerge feeling refreshed and rested.
3. Say a prayer of gratitude for the bath and for the clean water. A prayer of gratitude can be as simple as *Thank you for the bath*. Bring your palms together, and lower them to your chest (home of the heart chakra), pressing your thumbs into your heart center in a final prayer of gratitude.
4. Before you end your bath, close your eyes, and smell the scent of the soap or oil you are using. Listen to the water as you slowly move around. After the water begins to cool, prepare to slowly surrender your bath.
5. When you are ready, step out slowly and gently, and wrap yourself in a soft, dry towel. Slather lotion on your arms and legs and everywhere you want to retain moisture.
6. Before you slip into your pajamas, lift your arms up and over your head, gently arching your back while you enjoy a few more *Ahhhhh* breaths. Enjoy the feeling of being relaxed, scented, and rejuvenated.

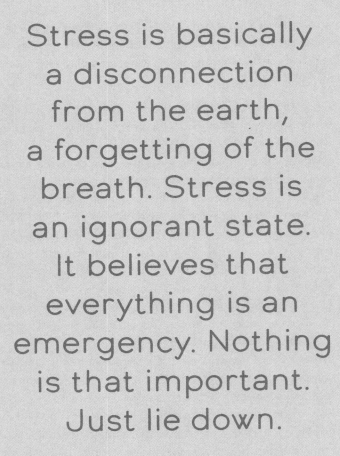

Stress is basically a disconnection from the earth, a forgetting of the breath. Stress is an ignorant state. It believes that everything is an emergency. Nothing is that important. Just lie down.

—NATALIE GOLDBERG
American author

Shine Your Heart Chakra

Your heart chakra or heart center is located in your upper chest, and is in charge of feelings of love and compassion, including compassion for yourself. It can be difficult to be at peace in your life if you are not feeling compassion for yourself, or are not able to connect with those around you with love. You can energetically send love and acceptance to yourself and those around you by getting in touch with the energy of your heart chakra, and "shining" that energy out to the universe. You can start by saying to yourself, *My heart is beating with peace and love.* While reciting this, imagine a beautiful pink light around your heart center. Allow this light to rest there while you breathe in and out. Feel the light as it sits on the front and back of your heart space, similar to how you might shine a flashlight. As you breathe, imagine this light growing stronger, radiating out in front of you, behind you, and alongside of you. Repeat your mantra, *My heart is beating with peace and love.* Imagine this mantra running through all chambers of your heart, creating a peaceful inner glow deep inside you.

Slide the Stress Off Your Shoulders

This breathing exercise helps you let go of the things that are causing you stress to give yourself the space and permission to relax and be calm.

1. Bring yourself to a comfortable seated posture on the floor.
2. With your eyes closed, think about who or what is on your shoulders, causing you to feel weighed down.
3. You may have your entire family lined up on your shoulders. Picture all of them there. What else or who else is on your shoulders? Friends, aging parents, relationship concerns, work responsibilities? Take time to really notice all of the people and "stuff" you are carrying.
4. Inhale into your belly. Exhale slowly; as you lean to your right, reach your right arm straight out and tilt over until your fingertips touch the floor.
5. Imagine everything and everyone sliding off your shoulders; "listen" joyfully as they scream *Wheeeee* while soaring down the slide that is your arm. Let them slip right off, trusting that they'll be fine, that they don't need to rest on your shoulders (and that you don't need them to rest there either!).
6. Inhale into your belly. Exhale slowly, and repeat the same motion with your left arm, letting everything and everyone on that side slide off. Give your arm a bit of a shake, as some people will (consciously or unconsciously) hold on really tight, even if everyone (especially you) knows it's best to let them go.
7. You can now fill up with calm and peace.

Create an Exercise Routine

Exercise may be one of the most perfect stress-management tools, yet it's often the first thing to go when our schedules get too busy. Setting up a regular exercise routine, and making exercise a priority, can keep you on track, and give you plenty of opportunity to burn extra tension and stress through physical activity. It's been scientifically proven that exercise helps improve mood; one way it does this is by boosting endorphins (brain chemicals related to mood). You'll be more likely to stick with an exercise routine when you enjoy the activity, so feel free to skip the elliptical in favor of a tai chi class or Pilates if that's your preference.

Adopt the pace of nature: her secret is patience.

—RALPH WALDO EMERSON
American poet and author

Pick Up a Textile Craft

The rhythm of clacking needles, the feel of soft yarn between your fingers, the persistent lull of the contiguous stitches, and the gentle pop as the needle pokes through the fabric—these are the sensuous pleasures of knitting, crocheting, cross-stitch, and other textile crafts that create space in your life to allow enlightenment to happen. The repetitive actions and soothing rhythms help you to take a break from thinking and worrying, and let you focus on the mechanics of your activity. You can learn these crafts with the help of a friend, a class, or online videos. The best part is that once you're done with your crafting meditation, you'll have a beautiful finished product to keep or to give away as a lovely, mindful gift.

Have a Good Laugh

Laughter is truly like medicine. It breaks up negativity, and calms your fears and anxieties. The laughing sounds of *ha* and *he* increase the movement of energy in your body. If you feel stressed or worried, take some time to watch your favorite funny movie or comedy special, a classic cartoon, or read through your favorite web comic. You can even search for funny Internet videos; there are hours of content compiled to make you giggle. Once you get a good belly laugh going, close your eyes and embrace that feeling of laughing very hard, deep in your belly. The power and positive energy of a good laugh can soothe negative emotions, and help you calm yourself down even after a very tough day.

Walk It Out

Whether you're walking outside your apartment or on your way to a meeting at work, take advantage of any random and precious quiet moments in your day to meditate. You can use this walking meditation to quiet your mind in general, or to calmly think through a problem that's been on your mind. It doesn't take any physical preparation; instead, it's a way to refocus your mind and the healing powers within it.

1. As you walk, visualize a question or problem you're stuck on.
2. Imagine it as a labyrinth and think of yourself as walking toward the center.
3. Cultivate gratitude. With each step you take, say *I'm grateful* with sincerity.
4. Focus on taking very slow steps. As thoughts unrelated to your focus come up, let them go.
5. As helpful thoughts come up, express gratitude for them. Continue walking until you have a solution, or until your mind is settled enough for you to sit down and get to business.

In the woods,
we return to reason
and faith. There
I feel that nothing
can befall me in life—
no disgrace, no
calamity (leaving
me my eyes), which
nature cannot repair.

—RALPH WALDO EMERSON
American poet and author

Imagine the Ocean

We humans have a natural affinity for water. During a busy day, this exercise can remind you of our roots in the ocean, and soothe your chaotic mind. You can perform it sitting or standing anywhere.

Start by closing your eyes and breathing deeply and regularly, concentrating on your breath, emptying your mind of all other thoughts. Then imagine that you are lying inside a glass-bottomed boat that is floating over the deep blue ocean waters. You are lying on your belly, looking down toward the ocean floor. There are many colorful fish swimming in the water beneath you. You are safe in the boat, yet you feel as if you are very much a part of the marine life—the coral reefs, seaweed, fish, and sea turtles. You can feel the boat rocking gently to the rhythmic motion of the ocean waves. A school of dolphins now appears. As they are swimming along playfully, they begin to breach the water near the boat, splashing salty water onto the deck. You are now wet and laughing. You slip out of the boat and are now swimming among the carefree dolphins. Any worries or concerns you have are fading away quickly as you immerse yourself totally into the fluidity of the ocean. You are filled with joy and peace, reveling in the moment. You are now floating on top of the water, looking up at the sky and basking in the feel of the sun on your skin. Slowly bring yourself back to shore as you bring your consciousness back to your body, carrying the peaceful feeling of the ocean along with you.

Do a Red Light Meditation

The next time you're in your car, use each red light as a reminder to take one full breath that you pay attention to the whole way through. Stop. Inhale. Exhale. How does it change your experience of your commute? Do you notice any difference in how you feel once you get out of the car and go on with your day? Finding quiet times in the day to remember to breathe can help you keep a calm, peaceful energy all day long.

We don't realize that, somewhere within us all, there does exist a supreme self who is eternally at peace.

—ELIZABETH GILBERT
American author

Breathe Like a Lion

The Lion's Breath breathing exercise in yoga, also called *Simhasana*, stimulates the nerves, senses, and mind, and energizes the immune system. It also relieves tension in the chest and strengthens the lungs. It's also amazingly refreshing and helpful for letting go of stress. Consider it like a big, aggressive *sighhhh* where you voice your frustrations and empty out all of the tension you've been holding inside. Avoid this breath if you have recent or chronic injury to the knees, face, neck, or tongue.

1. Sit in a comfortable position. Ground your weight down into your bottom and reach the crown of the head up to lengthen the spine. Take a moment to relax your body.
2. Close your mouth and notice your breath flowing in and out of your nostrils. Allow it to become steady and rhythmic.
3. Place your hands on your thighs with your fingers fanned out.
4. Inhale deeply through your nose as you draw your belly inward and press your chest forward, arching your upper back. Lift your chin, open your eyes wide, and gaze upward at the spot between the eyebrows.
5. Open your mouth and stick out your tongue. Stretch the tip of your tongue down toward the chin, and slowly exhale all of the breath out, while whispering a loud, strong *HAAAA* sound.
6. Repeat steps 4 and 5 four to six times. Then pause and relax. Close your eyes and let go as you feel the energy flowing through your head, eyes, throat, and belly.

Scan Your Chakras

Here's an exercise to bring your focus to all your chakras, or places of energy in your body; it's very helpful for calming yourself down.

1. Start your visualization at the root chakra, which is centered at the base of your spine. This chakra is about stability and grounding. Imagine the root chakra glowing bright red.
2. Next, visualize your sacral chakra, which is about 3 inches below your belly button. This is the chakra of emotions, including grief, as well as pleasure and creativity. imagine a bright orange color as you inhale and exhale.
3. Bring your attention to the solar plexus chakra, right at your diaphragm or upper belly. This chakra is about your inner strength and self-esteem. Imagine it with a bright yellow glow.
4. Move to your heart chakra, which is the center of your chest at about the height of your heart. This chakra is about love and compassion, for yourself and others. Imagine a vibrant emerald green glowing from your heart chakra.
5. Focus on your throat chakra, at the base of your neck. This chakra is about communicating and speaking your truth. Visualize it glowing blue.
6. Bring your attention to your third-eye chakra, at the center of your forehead. This is the chakra of insight, and it glows purple or indigo.
7. Finally, place your hands on top of your head at the crown chakra. Through your hands, visualize calming, healing white light flooding your brain. Feel yourself relax.

Try a Simple Breathing Lesson

You are taught many things as a child: how to tie your shoes, brush your teeth, and read and write. Breathing is not something most people are taught how to do, but luckily you do not have to be formally trained to learn how to breathe well. You can start right now by reciting this mantra. Take a long, slow, deep inhale (inflating your lower belly) and a slow, extended exhale (drawing your navel in), and recite this soothing phrase between each breath: *My breath is deep; my eyes are soft; I am at peace.* Do this for five rounds.

Peace comes from within. Do not seek it without.

—GAUTAMA BUDDHA

Sixth-century spiritual leader and founder of Buddhism

Enjoy Some Quiet Time

If you always have the TV or the radio on, or if you always fall asleep to the TV or to music, then you've probably got a noise habit. Noise can temporarily mask your loneliness or nervousness. It can calm an anxious mind or distract a troubled mind. Constant noise can provide a welcome relief from oneself, but if it is compromising your ability to think and perform as well as you could, or if it is keeping you from confronting your stress and yourself, then it's time to make some space for silence in your life. Too much noise is stressful on the body and the mind. Give yourself a break and let yourself experience silence at least once each day for at least ten minutes.

Take a Mental Vacation

What's the most relaxing place on earth for you? Is it in front of a fire in a mountain lodge, or on a hammock near the ocean? Close your eyes and imagine yourself there, wherever it may be. Really experience it—what can you see, smell, taste, and hear? How does your body feel when you're there? Because your brain can't perceive a difference between real and imagined relaxation, you can enjoy a truly restorative mini-vacation even if you can't hop a flight or take time off.

The more tranquil a man becomes, the greater is his success, his influence, his power for good. Calmness of mind is one of the beautiful jewels of wisdom.

—JAMES ALLEN
English author

Go Enjoy Nature

Doing a walking meditation outdoors is a great way to get in touch with your inner calm, and draw peaceful energy from the world around you, especially the green spaces that connect us with the calming energy of nature.

1. Choose a place for a quiet walk in nature—a nature path, a park, a tree-lined part of your neighborhood, or even your own garden; all of these will work, as long as you can see nature and feel natural energy.
2. Tread softly. Open your heart. Take a moment to be grateful for all of the blessings of everything that is good and beautiful in each moment and in each step that you take.
3. Notice the peace in your environment, and how nature reaches out to connect different things, like new vines creeping across old dead trees, or how green shoots grow between the cracks in the sidewalk.
4. Maintain a calm awareness of your body and your feelings as you walk.
5. As peace wraps around you, reach out with your own peace to send calm from your heart to others with the knowledge that your thoughts, intentions, and emotions are carrying a feeling of peace to whomever you choose to receive it.

Make a Calming Vision Board

You can use pictures of your friends, family, and your partner, as well as special memories, trips, and vacations, and combine them with pictures you pull from magazines or your favorite websites to create a calming collage. Create your own story. Make this activity mindful by reflecting on what the art says about where your heart is. If the collage shows things that you aspire to have or be, consider why you're not making them part of your life now. By taking the time to consider your past, what you love now, and where you dream of going in the future, you can stop obsessing over the daily stresses in the here and now and remember that you are blessed.

Create Your Own Sanctuary

As you go along in your busy day, it can seem impossible to find a peaceful moment anywhere. If you're feeling that way, try this meditation. It reminds you that you carry a sanctuary of calm within you wherever you go.

1. Sit up straight with your eyes closed. Begin by breathing deeply, concentrating your awareness between the eyes. You may see subtle lights, like electric sparks floating around. You may see mental formations, such as words and images, or you may see the outlines of your body or the room in which you are sitting.

2. Gradually move your center of awareness downward until it rests in the center of your chest. This may be a little difficult, because many people think of the head as the seat of consciousness. With a bit of effort, you should be able to remain in the chest region. Now begin to see this space. You may sense darkness, or you may visualize your heart and lungs expanding and contracting.

3. Now allow this area to fill with a white light tinged with violet. Picture this light as a countervailing force against the words and images in your head, just as the sun breaks through rain clouds after a storm. Make this inner vision stronger, until the light is extremely powerful.

4. After the visualization is established, stop trying to consciously produce it. Go back to simply observing. Realize that light and darkness are not opposites but part and parcel of the same reality.

Remember,
the entrance
door to the
sanctuary
is inside you.

—RUMI
Thirteenth-century Persian philosopher, theologian, and poet

Recline in Your Car

If you're feeling stressed or enduring mind chatter, here's a calming meditation you can do just about anywhere, as long as you have time to spare and your car available. Slide your seat back as far as it will go and recline. Bring your knees toward your chest, and place your feet on the dashboard (on either side of the steering wheel), or bring them up toward your chest, wrapping your arms around them. If you have one available, place a rolled towel or sweater behind your neck. If this doesn't work very well in your driver's seat, or if the posture leaves you feeling too exposed or vulnerable, move to the passenger side or the back seat. Once you are comfortable, notice your energy and your inner dialogue. If your inner dialogue feels judgmental (of yourself or others), visualize your breath entering the dialogue. Search for words that bring peace to you. They could be: *I can totally handle this new project* or *I am not responsible for everyone's happiness.* Think or say these words several times to see if they help shift your inner dialogue, and remember that even a tiny shift will bring you peace.

Cup Your Eyes

Here's a quick yet surprisingly effective meditation that can be done anywhere when you need to regroup and calm down.

1. Cup your hands over your eyes, enough so that you cannot see any light. Close your eyes and feel the darkness for a few slow breaths.
2. While your hands are still cupped over your eyes, open your eyes slowly. This may feel very peaceful. Imagine that you are in the deep shade, in the middle of a forest. Invite peace into your little "cupped" space.
3. When you feel peace entering and feel reassured that you are ready to handle whatever comes, remove your hands.

Anxiety does not empty tomorrow of its sorrows, but only empties today of its strength.

—CHARLES SPURGEON
Nineteenth-century English preacher and author

Remember That This Is Not Forever

This is especially helpful if you're fixated on a problem right now, and can't get away from the feeling of anxiety and the need to fix or get past the problem *now*. Remind yourself that this feeling and this situation aren't forever. See the inevitable ebb and flow of all things. Problems—and their solutions—are transient. They come and go like the rising and falling tides. When you see this rhythm in life, you're less likely to feel overwhelmed or trapped by your problems right now. Watch the clouds passing overhead, and imagine that each cloud is a problem in your life. Tag each one— unpaid bills, tight deadlines, piles of laundry, etc.—and watch it float across the sky and out of view. You can do this any time you find yourself stressing out over having too much to do or deal with—just close your eyes wherever you are, and imagine those clouds moving in and out of your mind.

Ground Yourself

Grounding yourself into the present moment is an essential part of transforming anxiety. Picture in your mind a large, old tree. See its strong root system and flexible branches. Picture the peacefulness of the tree and the nourishment it brings to its environment. You are no different than this tree. You also have a strong root system, capable of providing security and peace. Very often, when you are experiencing fear, energy becomes congested in the heart area and the solar plexus (navel area). To help your grounding, you can repeat this mantra: *Being firmly grounded into my body offers me peace.* When using this mantra, soften your solar plexus and when you exhale, imagine directing your energy out through your legs into the ground. See it travel through the earth, deep into the core of the planet. Allow this mantra to support your energy by grounding it into the earth through this tree visualization.

Anticipate Something Good

Anticipation is almost as much fun as the experience. Did you know that if you visualize a future event (or past event) in detail, as if it's happening in real time, your brain will believe that it's actually happening? That means that you get to enjoy the experience twice! If you're having a rough day, taking a moment to visualize something that will happen later that you'll enjoy—such as dinner with your family, or a movie with friends, or a long-awaited vacation—can really brighten your day. Build the visualization by coming to a quiet place. Then think about the details: Whom will you be with? Where will you be? What will you be doing? Imagine the tastes and smells and textures, the sounds and sights. If you're visualizing dinner with your family, imagine your children's faces as they tell you about the day or help you fix the meal. Feel the good feelings—as if they are already happening—and end your visualization by stating an intention to mindfully enjoy the upcoming experience...before transitioning back to your daily schedule.

Being relaxed,
at peace with
yourself, confident,
emotionally neutral,
loose, and free-
floating—these are
the keys to successful
performance in almost
everything you do.

—WAYNE W. DYER
American motivational speaker and author

Wring Out Your Stress

Every day brings with it a big to-do list. However, on those days when "too much to do" has escalated to an "insanely overbooked, overstressed, freaking-out" level, it's time to stop everything. That's right: don't do anything. Stop all thoughts. Stop the mind chatter. What you need to maintain sanity is to take a breather. This mindfulness meditation helps you stop and let go so that you're ready to tackle the insanity.

1. Lie down on a yoga mat or a rug. With your legs extended, take a few breaths, inhaling through your nose and exhaling a *Haaaa* out of your mouth.
2. Bring your knees toward your chest, and hug your knees for another few breaths, breathing normally.
3. Let your arms go out to the sides, and have your feet touch the mat with your knees bent. Inhale. As you exhale, bring your knees over to the right, and look to the left. Stay in this position for a few breaths. Then inhale, and exhale as you bring your knees to the other side and look in the opposite direction.
4. Think of your body as a giant kitchen sponge, and visualize yourself wringing out all of your chattering thoughts. Once you are "wrung out," you are ready to absorb quiet and peace.
5. Twist from side to side slowly, and as you do, exhale and wring out everything. If your mind resists and you are not able to stop the mind chatter, create the intention to replace the chattering with breath. Be patient with this intention, and remain in the meditation until you feel refreshed.

Stomp!

Stomping your feet is a great way to ground your energy and create a feeling of calm and stability. If you feel like you're carrying around a lot of negative, stressed-out energy, stomp it off! If you stomp outside, you leave the energy out there. Let it go. You can even stomp your feet outside each day after work before entering your home. Even if you love your job, there are daily annoyances you'll want to leave at the door; stomping them away allows you to keep work stress out of the house.

Spend Time with Your Pet

Studies have shown that owning a pet can reduce stress and provide excellent health benefits. If you spend just a few minutes petting your dog or cat, your mood goes up, blood pressure goes down, and breathing becomes more relaxed. Having a pet that needs to be walked means you are getting exercise too. A furry companion also offers a way for you to meet new people by going to a dog park. Today, spend some time with your pet. If you don't have one, ask a friend if you can take their dog for a walk or relax with their cat. Or consider adopting or fostering one from your local animal shelter.

The ideal of calm exists in a sitting cat.

—JULES RENARD
French author

Stop Trying to Be Perfect

Let go of your belief that you must be in charge of everything and everyone. The more persistently you hang on to your control issues, the more other people will resist—and resent—you. The next time you're about to panic over the imperfect state of your life, stop yourself before you start trying to fix anything—or anyone. Find a quiet corner away from the source of your panic—the messy kitchen, the uncooperative colleague, the unruly kids— and sit down. Make a list of the things you want to change: your roommate's untidiness, your colleague's bad work ethic, your kids' tantrums. Cross out whatever you cannot change. Hint: you can't change others; you can only change yourself. Now close your eyes and repeat the Serenity Prayer: *God grant me the serenity to accept the things I cannot change, the courage to change the things I can, and the wisdom to know the difference.*

Do Cobra Pose

Cobra Pose is a great energizing yoga pose for the middle of the day. The nature of the movements helps release whatever stress or fears have arisen, and restore your energy and calm. And because all you need is a wall, it makes a perfect office break.

1. Stand facing the wall. Place your hands at shoulder height and press them against the wall. Spread your fingers, feeling them press into the wall, and bring your elbows close to your rib cage.
2. Slowly lean forward until your body is pressed against the wall and your forehead is resting on the wall. (When you press your forehead onto the wall you will be stimulating the third-eye chakra.) Take a few breaths with your eyes closed. Inhale and press firmly into your hips. Exhale, lift your heart center as though you want to press it up toward the ceiling, and arch your back, letting your head reach back, opening your throat, and lengthening from your hips all the way up the front of your body. Think about the arch being in the upper back and not the lower back. Keep your neck long and not crunched.
3. Take a few breaths, and then on the exhale, bring your fore-head back to the wall. Do this "wall cobra" a few times until you feel better.

Have a Cup of Tea

Teatime is all about finding a quiet moment to take a breather. Lots of teas can contribute to a calm feeling: try something like chamomile or lemon balm. The warmth of the cup and the drink also help you to settle down, so feel free to substitute with cocoa or another warm beverage (you should probably skip the coffee, though, because too much caffeine might make it hard to slow down). Take the opportunity to turn the simple act of preparing your beverage into a meditative process.

1. Make use of all of your senses in your teatime meditation. Use your favorite teacup or even use your good china. Why not? Pampering yourself adds to the relaxation and refreshment you derive from a mindful meditation.

2. Pour the water into a teapot or directly into your cup. Let it sit for a few minutes. Lean over and smell the scent of the tea. Look at the color of the tea. Is it gold? Think about the color of gold. What does this bring up? Stay with positive thoughts: flecks of gold in your partner's eyes, the gold of a sunset or a summer flower, a gold ring, or anything that comes up.

3. Deeply inhale the scent of the tea and bring the cup up to your lips. Before you sip, pause to feel the warmth and breathe it in. Then slowly sip, using your taste buds and sense of smell to focus on the tea. What flavors are present? Can you taste flowers or herbs? If it's not too hot, hold a sip of tea in your mouth for a few seconds and truly savor the subtle flavors. Use all of your senses to enjoy your tea as though it were the first cup of tea you have ever experienced.

There is no
trouble so great
or grave that
cannot be much
diminished by a
nice cup of tea.

—ATTRIBUTED TO BERNARD-PAUL HEROUX
Basque philosopher

Call on Archangel Michael

Sometimes you need to call in the big guys when a stressful situation feels like too much to handle alone, and who better than the Archangel Michael to help defend your inner peace? He is a spiritual master and an archangel, and is the protector of those who call upon him. Michael has huge wings and a blue flame sword, and he stands ready to ward off anything that does not serve you. You don't need to be religious to call on him; he is available for all. You can call for Michael by saying some variation of: *Calling on Archangel Michael protects me and my loved ones now. Thank you.* When you do this, imagine him all around you (above, below, next to). Relax and feel his angelic presence. Avoid feeling like you are asking too much. His job is to protect you. And like most archangels, he respects you enough to wait for you to ask.

Get a Hot Stone Massage

If you've never had a hot stone massage, you are in for a one-of-a-kind experience. The stones are used in two different ways during the massage. One way is by providing heat to areas of the body to make the muscles relax and increase blood flow to speed up healing. They are usually placed along the length of the spine or along the chakra centers of your body. A towel will be between you and the stones, so don't worry about being burned. Another way the stones are used is as tools for deep tissue massage. Your massage therapist will cover the warm, smooth stones in oil and rub them on your body using long strokes in the area she is working on. This is an unbelievable sensation and one that helps wring out the stress you are carrying in your body.

Nothing gives one person so much advantage over another as to remain always cool and unruffled under all circumstances.

—THOMAS JEFFERSON

American Founding Father and third president of the United States

Ask Yourself What You Need

Stress can make everything feel urgent, which makes it hard to decide what to do next. Step out of the swirl by sitting still long enough to take a nice full breath, in and out. Then ask: *What do I most need right now?* Whatever answer bubbles up, resist the urge to question or dismiss it. Instead, honor it the best you can in this particular moment. Asking helps you see that you know more about what you need in any given moment than you might think you do.

Have a Drink

If you enjoy a glass of red wine, go ahead and pour yourself a glass as you cook dinner, or once you finally sit down at home after a long day; take a minute to mindfully notice the experience by savoring the taste, enjoying the deliciousness, and appreciating the luxury (even if it's an inexpensive wine!). Wine spritzers that mix wine with soda water are also fun. If you're making Mexican food, why not have a margarita or a mojito? Getting sloshed should not be the goal. The idea is to relax and enjoy something that gives you pleasure. If your spouse, roommate, or drinking-age family is at home, invite them to share a toast.

Listen to Music

You know that listening to music can lift your mood, give you energy, or take your edge off. You may not know that it can also be a health tonic—researchers have found a wide range of health benefits that result from listening to music, including altered perceptions of pain. Music also triggers the release of endorphins. Today, devote your full attention to a piece of music you love—during your commute, as you do the dishes, or as part of a wind-down routine before bed. Bonus points for singing along, as singing has been shown to reduce cortisol, a stress-related hormone.

✦

Music and
rhythm find
their way into
the secret places
of the soul.

—PLATO
Ancient Greek philosopher

Chop Your Way to Calm

When you're feeling particularly stressed, you can often feel it in your gut. This is because the body holds many emotions and stresses between the belly button and the rib cage (the third chakra, or solar plexus chakra). You can readjust this energy and shift it away from your stress center with a yoga pose and some breath work.

1. Take a minute to warm up your core: jog in place, walk around your room, or do a few jumping jacks to loosen up. Once you're finished, stand with your feet aligned with your shoulders at a distance of about a foot apart. Slightly bend your knees.
2. Press your palms together and raise your arms over your head. Think of your arms and hands working together as a big chef's knife, ready to smash down to break open a watermelon. Or you can picture this as a giant two-handed karate chop.
3. Exclaim *Ha* (the sound associated with the third chakra) loudly as you heave down your arms and hands in a single, swift movement to release emotional energy. Repeat until you feel emptied and calm.
4. Move your mat to the wall. Lie on your back with your legs up the wall, with your arms out to either side and palms open, and eyes closed.
5. Breathe away any remaining stress until you settle down and feel at peace.

Tune Out Drama

Interpersonal drama is created from conflict, insecurity, and pain, and it can be a huge roadblock to a calm and peaceful existence, especially if you get sucked into the fight. Perhaps you live in a family where gossip and conflict are common. Or maybe your workplace environment is like this. These types of family and/or work dynamics can get quite heated with tension. In an attempt to cope with the situation, you may be forced to detach yourself from it all. This may work to some degree, but tuning out or walking away is only a part of the process. See yourself as becoming neutral to what is happening. This means the drama does not impact you either way. In other words, you are able to observe without being drawn in.

Meditate On Water

This is a great meditation to do if you get a chance to spend time by a body of water, perhaps on a hiking or fishing trip, barbecuing by the local pond, or spending the day at the beach or lake, out boating on the water or lying on the shore. Walk around and see if you can feel watery. Move as if you had no bones. Feel fluid. Walk to a place to lie down. Close your eyes. Consider the healing properties of water, just in the functions of your body:

- Rivers of tears, sometimes pouring out of you, and at other times just a trickle.
- Tributaries of capillaries nourish every single part of your body. The flowing blood in your veins and arteries brings oxygen to every part of your body.
- The motion of your cells, the movement of your thoughts and feelings zipping around your brain—all the systems of your body are flowing.

Consider that you, too, are always flowing and changing. You can let the things that are bothering you flow away from you right now.

Be like a river. Be ever present and flowing.

—GURMUKH KAUR KHALSA

American yoga teacher

Release Your Tension

If you're still wired at the end of your day, you can try tense-and-release exercises to calm down. Begin by paying attention to your breathing. Is it fast or slow? Close your eyes, and breathe slowly in and out, drawing your breath into your tummy and then slowly blowing out all of the air. Then focus on each body part.

1. Start with your toes. Tense or curl your toes under, inhale, and then relax your toes as you exhale.
2. Tense your feet by pretending you are pointing your toes toward your forehead and pushing your heels away. Inhale while they are tense, and as you exhale, relax your feet.
3. Tense or squeeze your bottom and your entire legs, feet, and toes at the same time. Inhale, and as you exhale, release your bottom, legs, feet, and toes.
4. Pull your stomach in tight, until your rib cage is sticking out; bring your shoulders up to your ears. Inhale, and as you exhale, relax your tummy and your shoulders.
5. Clench your arms and your hands (making a tight fist), lifting them about 1 or 2 inches off the bed. Inhale, and as you exhale, relax your arms and hands, gently dropping them back on the bed.
6. Close your eyes really tight, and close your mouth really tight. Inhale, and as you exhale, relax your face.
7. Clench your entire body, including your bottom and face, and inhale. Hold this for a few seconds, and then, as you exhale, say a really long *Ahhhhhhhh.*

Be Here, Right Now

If you are feeling scattered or overwhelmed, reminding yourself to be present can help center you. True inner peace happens when you connect to the present moment. You can remind yourself with a simple mantra: *Be here, right now.* Before reciting this mantra, firmly plant your two feet on the ground. Picture them as roots of a tree anchoring into the earth. Now exhale into the core of your essence, drawing your belly button in, and whisper to yourself, *Be here, right now.* You can also add, *Peace. Peace. Peace.*

✦

No need to hurry. No need to sparkle. No need to be anybody but oneself.

—VIRGINIA WOOLF
English author

Adjust Your Posture

Neck and shoulder tension isn't just from mental stress; it's also a consequence of carrying your head out in front of your body (think of the typical sitting-at-the-computer position with your head craning forward). When your chin juts forward, your neck and shoulder muscles are forced to do the work of supporting your head that your spine is designed to do. To rediscover the ease that comes from proper alignment when sitting, gently slide your head back until the crown of your head is balanced atop your spine and level your chin. When you find the right spot, it should feel like relief. Whenever you notice that your chin has floated forward again (and it will—old habits die hard), don't take the bait to be hard on yourself for doing something "wrong." Simply allow it to glide backward once more.

Meditate On the Sounds Around You

Modern life is full of stressful, peace-disrupting noise—from the insistent electronic sounds of our computers and smartphones to the beeping of a microwave oven to the roar of traffic on city streets. Rather than try to block out all sound (which is unnatural and can trigger negative episodes), through this meditation you can determine how much sound you want to hear, and be able to take the sound in calmly and with pleasure.

1. In your most comfortable meditation posture, close your eyes. Begin to listen.
2. Start with the farthest sounds you can identify. For example, if you hear water running from a faucet down the hallway, listen to it to the exclusion of all else. The goal is to hear only the running faucet and nothing else.
3. Now go to the next sound that presents itself nearer to you. For instance, if you hear the wind blowing against the window of the room you're in, listen to it and exclude everything else.
4. Continue listening to sounds that are ever closer to you. Conclude with the sounds of your breath and your heartbeat.
5. Open your eyes and start again to listen to the sounds of your everyday life.

Say a Prayer of Gratitude

Sometimes the best way to be calm is to be mindful of the things you have to be grateful for. Sit quietly, close your eyes, and concentrate on one thing that you are truly thankful for right now. Hold this image in your mind, appreciating all the aspects that make you feel such gratitude and pleasure. Allow the feeling of gratitude for your many blessings to warm your heart. Breathe in and out slowly, quietly, enjoying the stillness of hearth and home. When you are ready, ask your higher power (God, the Divine, the creative spirit, or whatever spiritual reference holds meaning for you) to *Help me open my heart to a fuller understanding of myself and of my family. Give me the grace to walk on my own path to new growth. Amen.*

A tiny bud of a smile on your lips nourishes awareness and calms you miraculously.

—THICH NHAT HANH
Buddhist monk and author

Use Reiki

Reiki (pronounced *ray-key*) is an energy-healing technique based in ancient Tibetan practices. Practitioners of reiki put their hands on or just above the body in order to balance energy by acting as a sort of conduit for life-force energy. Reiki is used to treat physical problems as well as emotional and psychological issues, and it is, more positively, also used as a tool to support and facilitate positive changes. You can do self-treatments with reiki to help shift your energy, clearing out stress and creating space for calmness. As you place your hands, think of reiki flowing from the palms into your body, similar to the way in which water runs from a spigot into a basin. In doing self-treatments, imagine your body is the basin that needs filling, and the palms of your hands, facilitating the healing energies, represent the spigot.

Set an Intention

An intention is like a force field that you set around your thoughts—giving you a focus that keeps your mind from spinning in multiple directions. You can set an intention to remain resilient to stress and to keep calm throughout your day; or you can set an intention more specific to the challenges you are currently facing. To set one for yourself, create a simple statement about how you want to be (don't get too attached to a specific result, or else your subconscious may not buy it). Here are some examples of intentions you may want to set for yourself:

- Today, I'll stay curious when I get challenged.
- I'll look for the good in every situation.
- I'll find opportunities to do good.
- Whenever things get stressful, I'll have a safe harbor to return to.

Strive above
all else to
keep a calm,
restful spirit...

—FRANCIS DE SALES
Sixteenth-century Roman Catholic saint

Curl Into a Ball

In yoga, Child's Pose serves as a resting place between other more challenging poses, but it also makes a comfortable position for meditation. The pose itself reflects the position many babies take in the womb, and can help you tap into your inner reserve of calm. It also stretches out your back, right between the shoulder blades, where a lot of people carry their extra stress.

1. Come to your hands and knees. Inhale deeply, and when you exhale, lower your hips down to rest on your heels and flatten the tops of your feet on the floor. You can stretch your arms out above your head so that your palms rest on the floor, or you can stretch your arms straight down by your sides, palms up. Either way, close your eyes and keep your forehead gently resting on the floor. If this hurts your neck, you can put a yoga block or a folded blanket under your forehead.

2. Use this time to rest, recharge, and focus on your breath. Try focusing on breathing into the space between your shoulder blades, and opening that space further to new and calming energy.

3. When you are finished, come out of the pose slowly, coming back to hands and knees for a moment before rising.

How beautiful
it is to do nothing,
and then
rest afterward.

—SPANISH PROVERB

Visit a Zoo

The zoo is a great place to relax and enjoy the wonders of the animal world. This might be the only place you'll ever see lions or penguins up close. Go to your local zoo today. Many libraries offer discount tickets or coupons to local attractions—check with yours to see if you can get a discount for the zoo. Spending the day appreciating these incredible creatures helps you put things into perspective, and feel grateful for the wonders of our planet. Don't skip the informative signs throughout the zoo—read as many as you can so you walk away with something you never knew before about a species.

Do Some Gardening

There's something gratifying and soothing about taking care of plants, whether you're a master gardener or just trying to keep a houseplant alive. Having potted plants in the room has even been shown to help hospital patients recover faster. Take a break from your to-do list today to tend to whatever plants are in your life. Give them some water, clear out the brown leaves, get your fingers in the dirt. It will help you feel grounded and calmer. Digging in the dirt not only evokes the sense of child's play we experienced as kids in the sandbox, it also puts us back in touch—literally—with the earth.

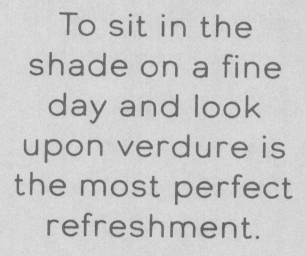

To sit in the shade on a fine day and look upon verdure is the most perfect refreshment.

—JANE AUSTEN
English author

Watch the Clouds

Clouds are nearly always present, yet they are always changing—just like your thoughts. Cloud-watching then can be a great way to develop some objectivity on the nature of your thoughts. Spend five minutes watching the sky—notice what the cloud shapes remind you of, see if you can detect movement or changes in appearance. Just as a massive bank of gray clouds will inevitably clear into blue sky, or a cloud shaped like a rabbit will morph into an ice-cream cone, your current thought pattern will also transform.

Try the Three-Part Breath

This breathing exercise is called the Three-Part Breath. When done with a focus on long, relaxed exhalations, it's especially good for calming the mind and nervous system. Avoid the Three-Part Breath exercise if you've had recent surgery or injury in your torso or head.

1. Sit comfortably with a long spine.
2. Seal your lips and relax your forehead, jaw, and belly.
3. Begin to take steady, long breaths in and out through your nostrils.
4. Let your breath slow down so much that you can feel your belly, rib cage, then chest expand and contract with each inhalation and exhalation.
5. Take a few minutes to establish a relaxed and even breathing rhythm.
6. Next, begin to slow down and extend your exhalations, allowing them to become longer than your inhalations. To help lengthen your exhalations, gently contract your abdominal muscles as you breathe out.
7. Without straining, draw your belly button back to the spine to create slow-motion exhalations.
8. Gradually build your exhalations to last twice as long as your inhalations. Stay relaxed as you gently contract your abdominal muscles to squeeze the air out of your lungs. Breathing this way helps to release strong emotions such as anger, frustration, and impatience.
9. Continue for three to five minutes.

Say *I Am Enough*

Very often, new beginnings can be looked at like a game of Monopoly—one wrong move and you are forced to go back to the start. For example, you might start a new business and then suddenly fear you don't have enough experience. Or maybe you are a new mother and suddenly feel overwhelmed by the responsibility. In times like these it helps to remind yourself that you are whole, and you are good enough exactly as you are. Take a moment and breathe in through your nose and out through your mouth. Slow down. Connect to your heart and state out loud: *I am enough*.

If in our daily
life we can smile,
if we can be peaceful
and happy, not only
we, but everyone
will profit from it.

—THICH NHAT HANH
Buddhist monk and author

Recite an Ancient Anger-Banishing Mantra

The words *Om Hrim Taha* (pronounced *aum hreem ta-ha*) mean "I cancel this heat (anger) in me through the energy of light." Anger can have many different expressions. Some people use the word frustration to describe their anger because frustration is a more socially accepted emotion. When it comes to this mantra, it does not matter whether you tend to lose your cool, hold in your anger, or express your anger in more passive-aggressive ways (e.g., saying *I'm fine*). As you recite it, trust that your body will respond and adjust itself according to your needs. For added benefit, you can center yourself through breathing and, if you like, add a visualization. In this case imagine yourself pushing the Cancel or Delete button on your computer, or turning off the heat on your stove. The sounds in this chant bring that heat right down so you can think clearly and act appropriately. Chanting this mantra when you are not angry makes it easier to memorize it. Then when you get heated up you'll be more likely to use it as a resource to help calm yourself down.

Take a Walk

Pick a place where you would like to walk—by a stream, on a path in the woods, by a fence, even a busy city street. No matter where you walk, you can use the time as an opportunity to engage in a walking meditation to create a bit of calm in your day. Keep in mind that you have no destination, just walking...that's it. Let go of any worries or concerns as you walk. Keep a smile on your face. Slow your walk to a stroll. This is not power walking. Let go of any agenda about walking, and focus on noticing the beauty of your surroundings. See things as if for the first time, as if you have been blind all of your life and now you can see. Notice all of the beauty that you see, from clouds in the sky to veins in a leaf, and really look at everything, surrendering all judgment. Let go of having to arrive anywhere and simply focus on enjoying the process of walking, surrounded by light and air and beauty. To keep the activity meditative, remember to keep returning your focus to your posture and your breath. If you like, you can bring your hands into prayer position and pause to express your gratitude for the beauty of your surroundings. Notice how peaceful and quiet your mind has become, and remember this feeling so you can tap back into it when things begin to pick up speed.

Say a Calming Mantra

Panic can feel like the rug is being pulled out from underneath your feet. Not all stress is bad, but sometimes you might carry a bit too much of it. If you feel panic, bring your awareness to your larger muscle groups (thighs and buttocks) and relax them. Begin to recite this mantra: *Now that I have released all excess stress, I am calm and peaceful.* Place your feet flat on the floor while you repeat the mantra. You may even want to rub the tops of your thighs with the palms of your hands, kind of like a massage, while reciting it. The combination of the mantra and connecting to your large muscles helps calm you down.

Have patience
with everything
that remains
unsolved in your
heart and try to
love the questions
themselves...

—RAINER MARIA RILKE
Bohemian-Austrian poet and author

Explore Touch

The sense of touch conveys a great deal of information that we might otherwise miss, if our sensory input was confined to the other four senses. According to yoga science, the sense of touch leads to understanding in a manner that regular learning cannot fulfill. Use this meditative technique to renew your sense of touch.

1. For this meditation, use clay, Play-Doh, or some other easily moldable material.
2. In your most comfortable meditation position, begin with your eyes open. Start with the hand you don't normally use. If you're right-handed, start with your left hand.
3. Work the material slowly. Press it and notice the reaction of the material. Give this a maximum of two minutes. Notice the material's response to you pressing it, squeezing it, and turning it. (Remember that you're not trying to create something here; rather you're investigating your sense of touch.)
4. When you stop, close your eyes. Take notice of the sensations in your hand. Start from the wrist and move outward to the palm. From the palm move to each finger in turn and move outward to the tip.
5. Open your eyes and practice this exercise with your other hand. If you want to continue the exercise, concentrate on arriving at the same degree of sensitivity and awareness in each hand.

Take a Yoga Class

Yoga classes come in many different flavors: some are restorative, some are created to make you sweat. But all of them help you to strengthen your connection to your body and to your energy, which is so important to keeping your reserve of inner calm. You shouldn't be intimidated by yoga; you can start slow, and learn to improve your technique as you stretch and strengthen your muscles and learn the proper feel of all the poses. Don't be too eager to achieve the "perfect" pose and correct bad posture habits immediately. It took a lifetime to get you where you are today. One yoga class won't change all that. In yoga, being present to each moment along the journey is more important than the destination—and it's also a lot more interesting!

✦

Each one has to find his peace from within. And peace to be real must be unaffected by outside circumstances.

—MAHATMA GANDHI
Indian activist and leader of the Indian Independence Movement

Say *Om*

The sound of *Om* is a universal mantra, the most often chanted sound among all the sacred sounds on earth. For most, a full-chested and slowly delivered *Om* replicates the sound of the vibrating and pulsating universe. Many also find the sound of *Om* a comforting sound, similar to home, mom, and amen. There is no actual meaning. It is not a word; it's a sound. It can be very effective in all kinds of situations, so experiment and have fun with it! It's also a great way to end meditations or yoga sessions, helping to connect spirit with mind and body.

Watch Your Favorite Scene

If you have some downtime, even if it's only twenty minutes, slide in your favorite DVD or search online for your favorite movie scene, and then sink your body into a comfortable position and let the story take your mind on a lovely side trip. This might work better if it's a story you already know well, so you won't feel compelled to watch to the end. If you know and love the story, you can pick and choose the specific portion. It might be a certain movie that can sweep you gleefully away, or it could be nature videos—watch whatever will leave you feeling refreshed and pampered. If you're at work and can take a short break, find something on the Internet that you'd love to watch for a few minutes.

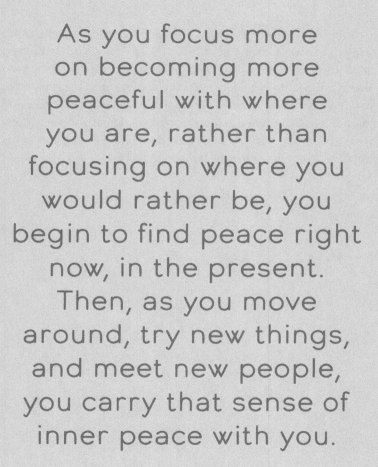

As you focus more on becoming more peaceful with where you are, rather than focusing on where you would rather be, you begin to find peace right now, in the present. Then, as you move around, try new things, and meet new people, you carry that sense of inner peace with you.

—RICHARD CARLSON
American author

Don't Do Things You Don't Want to Do

Growing up, you were likely told, "Sometimes you have to do things you don't want to." Which is true, but doing something strictly out of a sense of obligation, something that otherwise doesn't appeal to you at all, will only deplete you, stress you out, and make you feel resentful. There are no bonus points for being miserable. What's one thing in the next week that you really don't want to do at all? Can you simply not do it? (Or if it simply must get done, can you delegate it to someone else?)

Let Your Worries Float Away

This meditation walks you through a peaceful, calming visual, and helps you to imagine your worries drifting away.

1. Lie down if possible; if not, sit comfortably.
2. Imagine you are lying in the middle of a mountain meadow filled with wildflowers. Smell the earth, the fragrant flowers, the wild grasses. Feel the warm sun on your body. Listen to the sounds of birds in the distance, the humming of insects, the sound of the breeze rustling the trees.
3. Imagine that a mountain stream is off in the distance, and you can hear the movement of water.
4. Imagine all of your concerns, worries, hurts, and disappointments flowing down the stream like fallen leaves. Picture them floating away.
5. Each time a thought comes into your mind, let it flow down the stream. Let it go.
6. Become so still that all of your senses are alive.
7. Listen to the quiet sound of a fawn chewing young, green, wild grasses.
8. Relax, and let go of all thought.
9. Come to a place of peace, quiet, healing. When you feel calm at your center, stand up slowly, and take a short walk in your surroundings, reveling in the beauty around you.

Take a Time-Out

To give yourself a break and keep a leash on your frustration and stress, take this special time-out for yourself. Lean back against a wall, and press the back of your body toward the wall. Feel supported by the wall. Focus on your breath. Try to observe the flow of emotions. See if you can identify what emotion is present. Breathe into the emotion to see what is happening right now. Take a few more breaths. Consider the best way to handle the current problem. When you come to a place of peace and insight, you can return to the problem. Trust that you will know what is the best thing to do. As you come to a place of calm, those around you will feel it (even if they only feel it on a subconscious level) and will begin to feel calm as well.

Trees that
are slow to
grow bear the
best fruit.

—MOLIÈRE
Seventeenth-century French playwright

Do a Seated Forward Fold

Use your chair as a relaxation tool with this simple stretch that also quiets the mind.

1. Scoot to the edge of your seat, opening your feet and knees as wide as the chair seat.
2. Fold forward, resting your torso on your thighs, letting your head and arms dangle down toward the floor.
3. Stay here for a few breaths, feeling your rib cage inflate and deflate with each breath and imagining any stressful thoughts running out of your head and pooling onto the floor. So you don't disturb the peace you just created, roll up out of this slowly.

Blow Bubbles

Find a big bottle of bubbles, pull out the wand, pucker up, and blow! As you do, imagine that you are blowing your concerns into those self-contained spheres. Then watch them float up and away from you and out into the world where they can be absorbed into the atmosphere. This is a great exercise to use before a nerve-racking event—a big test or presentation, the first day of school—or at the end of a long day before starting your bedtime routine. Whenever you do it, do it with the intention of getting the stressors out of your head so that you can create space for more uplifting thoughts.

Do an Object Meditation

This meditation helps you quiet your mind and bring your focus back to you. Find an object that is beautiful or interesting to you. It can be a shell, a leaf, a religious symbol, or a piece of jewelry that has sentimental value—anything that is meaningful to you.

1. Place the object in front of you, positioned so that you are able to be seated with your eyes gazing forward at the object.
2. Keep your eyes focused on the object without looking away.
3. Begin to breathe deeply, transitioning into long, slow breaths that you draw deeply into your belly, slowly and fully.
4. Keep your every thought on the physical aspects of the object—the texture, size, color...all awareness rests on the physical aspects of the object. When your mind wanders, notice what it wanders to, and then bring it back to the object.
5. Once you feel calm and focused, close your eyes and try to "see" the object in your mind's eye. If you lose your concentration, open your eyes, study the object, and then try again. Stay with this meditation for at least five minutes, or as long as you'd like.

Do Downward Facing Dog

Because it stretches your entire back, strengthens your upper body, and improves circulation—all in a minute or less—the Downward Facing Dog yoga pose is a perfect way to refresh yourself and fight physical and mental stress. And because it literally changes your perspective, it helps reboot your thinking too.

1. To do the pose, start on your hands and knees.
2. Tuck your toes under, then straighten your legs and lift your hips up so you make the shape of an upside-down *V*.
3. Press strongly into your palms to move more of your weight back toward your heels, which are reaching down to the floor. Let your head dangle, its weight helping your neck and spine grow longer.
4. To make the pose more relaxing, rest your forehead (right at the hairline) on a stack of books or a yoga block. To make it more energizing, come forward into the top of a push-up position, or Plank Pose, as you inhale and move back into Downward Dog with each exhalation for a total of five cycles. Whichever form you choose, your back, neck, shoulders, heart, and mind will thank you.

For fast-acting relief, try slowing down.

—LILY TOMLIN
American actress

Let Your Problem Float Away

Think of a situation that's been weighing you down. Got it? Now imagine everything about this circumstance—your boss, your computer, the report you've been working on for weeks—all encased within a big balloon that you're holding the string to in your hand. And then see yourself letting go of the string and watching the balloon float up and out of sight. If you have trouble letting go, take an imaginary pair of scissors and cut that balloon string once and for all. When you find yourself thinking about this problem again, remind yourself that you've let it go.

Do the *So Hum* Chant for Peace

The *So Hum* chant is a traditional chant that's meant to reflect the sound of your breath—*So*: inhale, *Hum*: exhale. Focusing on your breath is a great way to find your calm in busy, hectic moments. You can do this while in a traditional yoga/meditation pose, or try it at your desk or another quiet place as you go about your day.

1. Sit cross-legged with a straight spine and palms resting up and open on your knees. Or sit in any comfortable position you can hold for a little while.
2. Close your eyes and focus your attention on the point between your eyebrows; do not strain.
3. Think the word *So* as you draw the breath in and *Hum* as you breathe out.
4. Keep your mind focused on that spot between your eyebrows (the third-eye chakra), and on your breath.
5. Notice how your shoulders relax and your tension slowly ebbs away. *Ahh!*

Try a Tai Chi Exercise

You can tell yourself to "let it go" all you want, but sometimes you need a physical practice to make that release tangible before your mind can loosen its grip. Here's one from tai chi: Stand with your feet shoulder-distance apart, knees slightly bent, arms hanging loosely by your sides. Feel your body from the waist down dropping into the floor, and from the navel up extending up toward the sky. As you inhale, sweep your arms out and up to chin height, palms facing forward, as if you were going to give an invisible person a hug. As you exhale, bend your elbows and bring your fingertips toward each other, turning your palms to the floor, and slowly move your hands and straighten your arms down toward the floor, as if you were pushing them through water. Imagine this downward sweep pushing any stress or toxic energy from your body into the ground where it can be absorbed. Repeat three to five times.

◆

Life is a series of spontaneous changes. Don't resist them—that only creates sorrow. Let reality be reality. Let things flow naturally forward in whatever way they like.

—LAO TZU
Chinese philosopher and founder of Taoism

Listen to Your Body to Keep Your Cool

Part of learning how to approach life with calm is learning how to listen to your body's cues. When the hair stands on the back of your neck, or you feel an urge to move away from someone, trust these senses. Likewise, if you're trying to take on too much in your schedule, stop and listen to what is right for your body so as to create balance. Remember, your body has your back, so you should trust the little voice inside your heart sometimes (not your head). Your body has something valuable to tell you. Trust it.

Have a Meal with Friends

If you've had a tough week, one involving a lot of frustration and little pleasure, change up your energy by spending time with people who make you feel at ease. Get on the phone, and see if your friends would like to pool resources and come up with something edible, or join you for takeout. For these occasions, no matter what you eat, set the table and make it an occasion. Light candles, put flowers in a centerpiece, bring out the good wineglasses, and act as if you're eating filet mignon or lobster. When your guests show up, stop everything you are doing and greet them at the door. Give each of your guests a really big hug, bringing your hands onto the back of their heart centers. Or if you're not a hugger, you can simply greet each guest individually. This way you'll all feel special, which is guaranteed to boost your spirits.

Perform a Body Scan

An important way to bring yourself into the present moment, and to release any stress or tension you're carrying in your body, is to do a body scan. The idea is to sit or lie down and place your attention on one body part at a time. Then you can relax each part one by one.

1. Lie on your back, with your legs outstretched comfortably on the floor. Place a pillow or cushion underneath your knees. Do not put a pillow underneath your head.

2. Take a slow, deep inhale through your nose and exhale through your mouth. Let go. Feel yourself supported by the ground, by the earth. You are held; you can let go. Pay attention to your breath flowing in and out for a few breaths.

3. Then turn your attention to your right foot. Notice your toes; relax the entire foot. Relax the right ankle. Feel your entire right leg. Relax the right leg. Notice the right side of your torso. Relax the right side of your torso. Relax the right shoulder. Relax the top of the right arm; relax the forearm. Relax the right hand, including the right fingers.

4. Notice your left foot. Relax the toes; relax the entire left foot. Relax the ankle. Feel your left leg. Relax the entire left leg. Draw your awareness to the left side of your torso. Relax the left side of your torso. Relax the left shoulder. Relax the top of the left arm; relax the forearm. Relax the entire left arm.

5. Relax the lower back. Relax the middle of your back. Relax the shoulder blades. Relax the neck. Relax the jaw. Relax the tongue. Relax the eyelids. Relax the temples. Relax the brow. Relax the entire head.

Let peace
be your
middle name.

—NTATHU ALLEN
American yoga and meditation teacher and author

Bake Your Own Bread

With just a few simple ingredients, you can have a warm loaf of bread baking in your oven, making the house smell delicious and giving you a peaceful sense of accomplishment. Look for recipes online or in a cookbook. If this is your first time making bread, start with an easy recipe. Be sure to pick up bread flour and yeast at the grocery store. To make your life easier, invest in a bread machine. These wonderful gadgets can mix, knead, and bake a loaf of bread in about three hours. Or you can mix and knead by hand, which could help you muscle out some additional stress! Make your favorites like white, wheat, rye, and pumpernickel. Or try cinnamon raisin for breakfast or garlic herb when you are making an Italian dinner. There's nothing like the smell of fresh-baked bread to make your home feel warm and inviting. Once you start making homemade bread, you'll never want to eat store-bought bread again.

Remember That You're In Control

People who are anxious or stressed can often feel trapped by situations in their life: feeling stuck means you believe you have limited choices. Listen to the words you use to describe your situation. If you hear yourself saying statements such as *I have to* or *I should*, then it is likely you are feeling powerless. But you always have the power to move whatever obstacle you believe is in your way. If you're feeling stuck, try this exercise. Recite the following phrase: *Choice is freedom. I choose to* _____. In the blank, fill in an empowering statement. For example, rather than saying *I have to go to work*, instead say *I choose to go to work*. Then add how this choice benefits you: *By going to work I can afford a nice place to live, good food to eat, and hobbies I enjoy*. Or instead of *I have to go to the gym*, you can say *Choice is freedom. I choose to go to the gym so I can be healthy and look good at my high school reunion*. This phrasing gives you more energy and puts you back in the driver's seat as a co-creator of your life experiences, and helps reassure and calm you when you feel powerless.

Be Realistic about How You're Feeling

The next time someone asks how you are, resist the urge to say *fine* or *busy* and share something that feels true for you at that very moment: hungry, irritated, distracted, happy for no apparent reason, a little punchy. This gives you an opportunity to check in and see how you're really doing. Suppressing your feelings or not being honest about them creates a bottleneck, where your stress just builds and builds without any release. Being honest allows you to let off some of the pressure of whatever is bothering you. It also creates an opening to truly connect with the person who's asking—she'll likely be surprised by your answer and will want to either hear more or think a little more deeply about her response when you ask, *And how are you?*

Watch Your Breath

This breathing exercise is sometimes called *Shamatha* with support. *Shamatha* means "calm abiding, tranquility, or meditation." All we are doing is watching breathing—no more, no less. This breath watching will, with even a few minutes, calm the nervous system and bring a feeling of peace. Close your eyes. Close your mouth. Take a few minutes to pay attention to your breath.

1. Notice the length of each in-breath. If your in-breaths are only two or three seconds long, they are shallow breaths, a surefire sign that you're stressed.
2. Notice the direction of the breath. When you inhale, can you feel the breath filling your lungs and causing your belly to expand? Can you feel the breath entering your nose and cooling the inside and then passing downward into your lungs?
3. After bringing all this awareness to the breath as it is, slowly begin to inhale longer and deeper. You want each in-breath to be about five or six seconds long and the exhale to be an equal length of time.
4. Bring your right hand to your belly. Breathe deeply (five or six seconds), drawing in air until your belly presses into your hand. As you exhale, let your navel sink until it is pressing toward your spine.
5. Continue breathing in and out as you begin to count the breath: 1, 2, 3, 4, 5 for the in-breath and 5, 4, 3, 2, 1 for the exhale. If counting seems too boring, say a mantra, such as *May I have peace* as you inhale and *May all have peace* as you exhale.

Send Love Your Way

Overfocusing on your problems or worrying about the future disables your ability to tune in to love and self-acceptance, and to find your inner peace right now. Rather than continue these patterns, choose to focus on self-love. Self-love is not as complicated or overwhelming as you might think. The act of pausing and taking a drink of water is a demonstration of love. Noticing the temperature of the water as it runs over your hands while washing dishes is a way to connect to love. Love is in the moment; it is right now, as you are reading this. Pay attention to how your body responds to the experiences and interactions of your day without judgment. Soak up moments that offer you connections to the moment. These are all part of love.

✦

Anxiety's like
a rocking chair.
It gives you
something to do,
but it doesn't
get you very far.

—JODI PICOULT
American author

Stop Defying Gravity

Being pulled in a dozen different directions by people, work, and responsibilities can take a toll on your peacefulness. This meditation reminds you to reconnect with the natural forces that are in play around you, all the time, and helps you to let go and stop fighting against the energies of the universe.

1. Find a place where you can lie flat on the floor without being disturbed. Turn off the light. If you feel any discomfort, place a cushion beneath the small of your back, behind your knees, or under your neck.

2. Set a timer for five minutes. Practice deep, slow breathing. Become conscious of gravity pulling your body into the floor. Imagine gravity pulling any tension out of your body and pulling away disturbing thoughts as well. Become one with the floor beneath you, and imagine yourself to be an inanimate part of the floor. Pretend that you have forgotten how to speak, either to yourself or out loud.

3. Allow yourself to rest in a state as close to mindlessness as you can achieve. When the timer sounds, try to take some of this interior silence with you.

Get Spiritual

Whether or not you have religious beliefs, you can still appreciate the power of spirituality. Think of it as the part of you that can't be measured, calculated, or wholly explained—the you that makes you *you*. When we ignore our spiritual side, we throw our bodies out of balance. When our spiritual lives are further compromised because of the effects of physical and mental stress—low self-esteem, anger, frustration, pessimism, the destruction of relationships, the loss of creativity, hopelessness, fear—we can lose the energy and joy of life. If you are struggling to feel calmer, get in touch with your spiritual side, and reach out to a higher power for support. Your higher power can be a religious figure, the power of the earth, or the energy of the universe: it helps to unburden yourself to a power that is greater than you.

That's what I call meditation. You simply stand aloof and just see the mind disappearing, like a cloud on a faraway horizon, leaving the sky clean and pure.

—OSHO
Indian religious leader and mystic

Say a Traditional Chant for Peace

Recite the words *Om Shanti* (pronounced *aum shh-aunt-eee*). This translates to "Infinite consciousness for peace, calm, and bliss for everyone everywhere." The word *shanti* can mean "peace, bliss, and calm" for everyone in every way. Tradition recommends that this Hindu chant be repeated a minimum of three times. One for the body, one for speech, and one for the mind. This chant removes anything interfering with peace. Use it to cleanse the words that come out of your mouth. You can also chant *Om Shanti* before sending an email or text, making a phone call, walking into a store, or tending to a task. See it as removing anything that might disturb peaceful interactions.

Let It Go with a Mantra

Peace can be difficult to find if you're plagued by regrets, or "stuck" dealing with a problem or person you just can't get out of your head. In these cases it's best to just let go of the worry, and the situation, so that you are free to move on. This is easier said than done, but repeating a mantra can help. The next time you hear yourself saying "I need to move on" or "if only I could just stop thinking about this person or situation," consider reciting this mantra: *I choose to let go by moving in rather than moving on.* When it comes to forgiveness, there is no moving on; there is only moving in. Your attitude and life experiences may change, but it is only when you move deeper into yourself that you will truly be liberated. Allow the mantra to draw your awareness inward. As you move inward, your perception will shift and you may realize that there was never anything to let go of in the first place. The thing you thought you needed to let go of turns into something you have learned to appreciate and respect.

Watch the Tides Change

One of the most amazing things that happen on earth every day is the changing of the tides. The tides are controlled by the gravitational pull of the moon; they go in and out a number of times during the day. Tides can help us remember that everything in life is cyclical and always changing. What troubles us today will pass. The sounds and smells of the ocean can be soothing as well. Head down to the beach today to watch the tides change. You can check the newspaper or go online to read the tide charts, those handy daily updates that let you know when the tides go in and out. Bring a chair so you can sit right at the water's edge. The tides change slowly, so enjoy your time with your feet in the water.

Do not let the behavior of others destroy your inner peace.

—TENZIN GYATSO
His Holiness the fourteenth Dalai Lama

Let Go of What Keeps You from Being Calm

This meditation helps you release worry so there's room for you to be calm. Some days you may find that even this meditation doesn't work—your worries just won't go away. That's okay too. Simply accept the worries as they are. With practice it will become easier to let the leaf float downstream.

1. Sit up straight on the floor, on a mat or a blanket.
2. Breathe deeply through your nose, or through your mouth if that's not comfortable.
3. Straighten your legs in front of you, and flex your feet by pressing your toes toward your forehead; feel your hamstrings stretch.
4. Lean forward without bending your knees. Come to your edge, that point where the stretch is uncomfortable but just short of painful, and stay for a few minutes.
5. Try closing your eyes. Notice any physical, emotional, or mental experiences you may be having, such as experiencing a tight hamstring, or feeling overwhelmed, or worrying about something happening in your workplace. Each time a thought or emotion surfaces, try to replace it with a breath. Or you can envision a stream and picture each thought or sensation or emotion as a leaf floating by. For example, you may be in your posture and realize that you are planning dinner in your head. Look at this thought, and let it float by, down the river.

Create a Ritual

You can ward off stress by creating a ritual that nourishes you and that you do every day, even if five minutes is all you can find. It could be pruning flowers in your garden, enjoying a glass of lemonade while sitting in your backyard, going online to find a recipe you're dying to try, or calling your mother, best friend, or husband. Maybe you can find a quiet nook where you can light a candle and sit to write in your journal. Or maybe you'd prefer blasting a song from when you were in high school, and dancing like a maniac. It could be absolutely anything that pleases you, as long as it reminds you that you need a little pampering too.

Take a Calming Shower

Taking a shower provides a few minutes for you to focus on yourself: the gentle pressure and the warmth of the water can soothe away your stress and help you to calm down, either as you get ready to take on the day, or as you recover and refresh from your busy day. You can make your shower even more peaceful by making it a mindful shower. Clear your mind of any distractions, and then move slowly, enjoying each sensation as it occurs. If it helps, state your intention clearly: *I am shedding all my worries to focus on my body and my senses.*

1. Begin by stepping into the shower. Stand still for a few minutes, letting the water run over you, quieting all thoughts, experiencing the rejuvenating powers of warm water.
2. Turn your attention to your feelings. How does it feel to have peace and quiet? Breathe in relaxation, and breathe out frustration. Notice as worries dissipate and how it feels when muscle tension subsides.
3. Pay attention to your senses: smell the fragrance in your soap or shampoo, and feel the rough texture of your scrub brush. Allow the smells and textures to conjure up pleasant memories. Listen to the water as it cascades over your head and hair. Listen as the drops of water strike the shower curtain or the glass.
4. Toward the end of your shower, take a few really deep breaths, saying *Ahhhhhh* as you exhale.
5. Stay focused on sensations as you climb out. Notice the texture of the towel you use to dry yourself. Notice how it absorbs the water, how clean your dry skin feels against the towel.

All the trees
are losing their
leaves, and
not one of them
is worried.

—DONALD MILLER
American author

Melt Away Your Resistance

"What you resist persists." In other words, if you resist feeling free and at ease, your body will learn how to remain in a state of resistance, and you will feel tense and alert, unable to be really calm. This is fine if you are truly being threatened, but you are not meant to be in a state of resistance for very long. Resistance holds a congested, heavy energy. You can let go of resistance in your body by imagining your resistance melting like a Popsicle in the sun. As you picture the details of this scene, repeat to yourself, *All resistance melts freely from me now.*

Repeat a Word

Dr. Herbert Benson coined the term "relaxation response" in 1975, when he published the book *The Relaxation Response*. Benson suggests picking "a focus word, short phrase, or prayer that is firmly rooted in your belief system" to help trigger your relaxation response. Choose a word to symbolize what kind of energy you wish to take in, such as peace, calm, unity, or love. Say the mantra, *Breathing in* (then inhale) *and breathing out* (and exhale). Then recite your word, and relax the muscles in your face and body while breathing in and out through your nose, slowly filling up your lungs (inflating abdomen on inhale and deflating on exhale). The word helps you to focus your awareness while concentrating on your breathing. That's the relaxation response.

✦

Any idiot can face a crisis—it's this day to day living that wears you out.

—ANTON CHEKHOV
Nineteenth-century Russian playwright and author

Pause and Reflect

The next time something really gets you riled up, try this: First, notice that you're steamed. (Awareness is always the first step in doing things differently.) Then stay open long enough to ask questions (before you start yelling or firing off snippy emails) such as: *What's really triggering me here? Is there some other way I could interpret this? What if this has nothing to do with me?* When you can manage to tap into curiosity, you're less likely to judge something as right or wrong, good or bad. As a result, you're less likely to overreact, which can create an even more stressful situation.

Lie in *Savasana*

Taking a restorative midday break can help you reduce stress and stay healthy and available for your family. The purpose is not to really sleep, but to rest your body and mind. A nap in the yoga pose *Savasana* has the added benefit of reminding you to be mindful as you relax and refresh yourself. *Savasana* typically is practiced at the end of a yoga session as a way to rest the muscles (and the mind!) while allowing the poses just completed to work their magic, but it's also a great way to quiet your mind and body and practice a refreshing silent meditation.

1. Corpse Pose, or *Savasana*, is done while lying flat on your back on a yoga mat or a rug. Many find it more comfortable to place a bolster, rolled towel, or pillow under their knees. A folded hand towel or a scented eye pillow placed over your closed eyes will help you relax further. Some people like to play soothing instrumental music while taking a *Savasana* rest.
2. To begin, bring your arms straight down by your sides. If you are cold, bring your arms close to your body, and if you are warm, move your hands about several inches or more away from your sides. You can cover yourself with a soft blanket if you'd like. Remember, the intention is not to fall asleep but to calm your body and mind. If you fall asleep, that's okay too; that is what your body needs in this moment.
3. When you feel rested (or when your music or timer cues you that the time is over), roll to your side, come up slowly, pause to take a few deep, cleansing breaths, and then open your eyes.

Listen to Your Heart

Many people have been told to do one thing, but their heart steered them to another. If something feels right in your heart, it probably is right for you. In your mind you may doubt your choices or abilities, but your heart usually gently tugs you back to what feels right. Go with this. Listen. Trust that your heart knows the way to consciousness. Your heart is highly intelligent. The more you listen, the stronger your ability to do what feels right will come through, and the less you have to worry about making the "right" decision. The right decision for you is the one that will bring you the greatest contentment, and when you follow your heart you are much more capable of pursuing your own inner peace.

Let Go of a Grudge

One way you likely contribute to your life feeling stressful is by holding on to things like grudges, hurts, and narratives about how you were wronged. (How very human of you!) The problem is, as righteous as they may make you feel, these unresolved feelings take up space and zap energy. It's like carrying around a backpack full of rocks. Sure, you're capable of doing it, but what do you get out of it? What's one small rock you can set down? What trespass can you forgive, or what story can you spin a different way? It's not about letting someone else off the hook, but about letting go of energy that's keeping you from feeling calm and peaceful.

Give Yourself an
Aromatherapy Massage

Essential oils are mindfulness tools that can enhance mental clarity and relaxation. You can put them directly on your body, add them to your bath, or use them in a diffuser. To be most effective, essential oils should be pure and uncut. Essential oils need to be diluted in a base carrier before being applied to the skin. A base carrier oil is a pure oil, such as extra-virgin cold-pressed olive oil or sesame oil, that can be used to dilute essential oils. Get the best carrier oil that you can, from a specialist store. What you put on your body gets absorbed into your body, so you want only the purest and best oil when you apply it to your skin. Then add drops of the essential oil to the base carrier. A typical recipe is to measure the amount of base oil in milliliters and then divide that number in half to give you the maximum number of drops of essential oil that you will need. After testing the oil on the skin to make sure there is no allergic reaction, you can do a healing self-massage. First, put a couple of drops of the mixture of base oil and essential oil onto your hands, and rub your hands together to stimulate the scent of the oil. Bring the palms of your hands up to your face, and inhale the scent for several breaths. Then, gently begin to massage the top of your head, at the crown. Next, slowly progress down the body, giving every part of you the attention it deserves. Continue to inhale the aroma that gently wafts through the air. When you've finished with the massage, relax. Allow the effects of the massage to sink in. Envision the healing occurring. Enjoy the process!

It's not time to worry yet.

—HARPER LEE
American author

Chill Out with the Moon

This breathing pattern is called Lunar Breath. By directing the breath through the left nostril, which is associated with the cooling energy of the moon, the mind and body become soothed and relaxed. You can picture the moon while you do this exercise: see its gentle glow, and the soft white craters. If you suffer from low blood pressure, colds, flu, or any other respiratory conditions, avoid this breath exercise.

1. Sit comfortably with a long spine.
2. Hold up your right hand and fold your index and middle fingers into the palm of your hand, keeping the thumb, ring finger, and pinky extended.
3. Seal your right nostril with your thumb and take a slow and complete breath in through your left nostril.
4. Seal your left nostril with your ring finger, release your thumb, and exhale out of the right nostril.
5. Repeat this sequence—inhaling through your left nostril and exhaling through your right.
6. Continue for three to five minutes.

Stop Thinking

Whenever you're feeling overwhelmed, you can calm yourself down and declutter your mind with this simple, quick meditation. The idea of this meditation is "nonthinking": emptying all the thoughts that sprang to attention and started marching around your brain the minute you woke up. Take at least a few minutes to simply be still and quiet your mind, and the reassurance, energy, and peace that you need will come.

1. Find a quiet place where you can have some privacy.
2. Sit on the floor or in a chair. You can sit with your legs crossed or straight out in front of you, however is most comfortable for you.
3. Once you are in this position, slowly straighten your spine, raising the crown of your head toward the ceiling and tucking your chin in slightly. Relax your shoulders.
4. Close your eyes or just lower your gaze.
5. Relax your hands onto your knees, palms up.
6. Inhale slowly through your nose, and exhale slowly through your mouth.
7. Spend several minutes doing nothing except focusing on your breath. If thoughts arise, do your best to ignore them, or silently acknowledge them without judgment, and return your attention to your breath.
8. When you feel centered, calm, and grounded in your being, release and slowly stand. Take this feeling of calm with you through the rest of your day.

Index